"*Romantic Intelligence* is the glue for someone looking to piece together the shards of their emotional life. Our emotions provide us with a sophisticated and fragile inner guidance system. We put up roadblocks to this network, relying heavily on our intellect rather than our heart to solve life's questions. By the time you put this book down, Mary and John Valentis will have taken you on a journey from lost-in-love to a fulfilled life with the fluidity of their words and direct language."

> —Amanda Bird, US National Skeleton Team member, 2003 Summa Cum Laude graduate, University at Albany

"As a 'book-smart woman,' I found my bad relationships a painful cauldron for learning about love. *Romantic Intelligence* offers clear, commonsense observations that would have greatly shortened my journey toward romantic health."

> —Kathlyn Hatch, Designer/Educator

ROMANTIC
INTELLIGENCE

How to Be as Smart in Love as You Are in Life

Mary Valentis, Ph.D.
John Valentis, Ph.D.

New Harbinger Publications, Inc.

Publisher's Note

Distributed in Canada by Raincoast Books

Copyright © 2003 by Mary Valentis and John Valentis
New Harbinger Publications, Inc.
5674 Shattuck Avenue
Oakland, CA 94609

Cover design by Amy Shoup
Edited by Kayla Sussell
Text design by Michele Waters

ISBN 1-57224-330-9 Paperback

New Harbinger Publications' Web site address: www.newharbinger.com

05 04 03

10 9 8 7 6 5 4 3 2 1

First printing

John dedicates this book to his friend Sylvia Thaler.

Mary dedicates this book to her friend Shirley Belden.

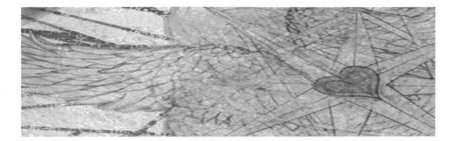

CONTENTS

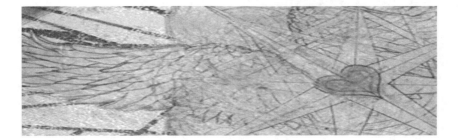

ACKNOWLEDGMENTS

Book ideas float out of the sky, hang around in the air, and permeate your sleep in that hazy time just before you wake up. But not this one. The idea for this book was etched on a Nantucket Island beach many years ago when the late Marta Greene picked up a stick and drew a circle in the sand that diagrammed how romantic couples ideally pair up and how compatibility really works. Those memorable conversations with Marta on 'Sconset Beach, and talks during extended walks with two other women friends (who know who they are), prompted the creation of a class on romantic love, more reading and experiencing, and finally coming together with John when both of us discovered how transformative and mutually supportive romantic relationships can be and continue to be.

Phillip has taught Mary how to love from the beginning and he, Tom, Barbara, Arthur, Carey, and, hopefully, Wendy complete the circle of love. John's patients and Mary's students inspire, teach, and awe us every day.

We would like to express our admiration for and appreciation to our colleagues and collaborators at New Harbinger Publications: Jueli Gastwirth who shepherded this book through its acquisition and developmental stages along with Heather Michener, our editor Kayla Sussell whose expertise and practiced eye honed and shaped our words into the final elegant filament, and Lorna Garano, an extraordinary publicist. The following friends, family, role models, lovers, strangers, and romantically intelligent couples have inspired and contributed to this book in immeasurable ways: Claudia LeMarquand and John Burdy, Peter and Ira Mendleson, Toni and Irvin Thompson, Hal Sporborg, Bill Hedberg, Dana and Bill Kennedy, Maggie Mancinelli, Laurie Jacobson, Louise and Larry Marwill, Sandra and Stewart Ray, Elena Vaida, Phoebe and

Matt Bender, Jean Bender, Bea and Bob Herman, Rena and Dan Button, Bea and Sol Greenberg, Tom and Agnes Naughton, Glenn Veen and Beatrice Landolf, Joan Wick-Pelletier, Donna Cooper, Pat Walker, Janis Kent, Joan Curry, Brandi Ingersoll, Diana Roschko, Carline Davenport, Amanda Butler, Jodi Renner, Mimi Netter, Arvilla Cline, Betty Nathan, Lucille Stein, Marcia Scharfman, Charles and Xenia Stephens, Charles Anderson, Kathlyn Hatch, Rose and Paul Patrinos, Cousin Eppy, Bob Sager, and John Gillespie.

Finally, we owe a great debt to Daniel Goleman whose wonderfully researched book, *Emotional Intelligence,* recast the idea of what it means to be smart in life, and provided the theoretical foundation for applying the basics of emotional intelligence to romantic relationships. We are also indebted to Princeton-based family therapist Maggie Clune, Dr. Lloyd Glauberman, and Dr. Richard Mastrodonato whose expertise guided us in defining romantic intelligence.

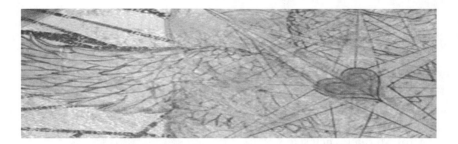

ARE YOU AS SMART IN LOVE AS YOU ARE IN LIFE? TEST YOUR ROMANTIC INTELLIGENCE

1. Love at first sight happens: ____
   (a) All the time
   (b) Rarely
   (c) If you're looking for it
   (d) Never

2. The difference between love and infatuation is: ____
   (a) There is no difference
   (b) Infatuation is more romantic
   (c) Love involves more of the total person
   (d) Love is more honest

3. Romantic intelligence starts with: ____
   (a) Self-awareness
   (b) A college education
   (c) Sexual experience
   (d) Romantic experience

4. It's better to conduct your love life with: ____
   (a) Your heart
   (b) Your head
   (c) A combination of both
   (d) Without any preconceptions

5. Compatibility today is based more on: ____
   (a) Religious and ethnic backgrounds
   (b) Emotional levels
   (c) Educational levels
   (d) Economic levels

6. Sexual intimacy and emotional intimacy are: ____
   (a) The same
   (b) Mutually inclusive
   (c) Mutually exclusive
   (d) May exist both with and without each other

7. The smarter you are in school, the better you will be at: ____
   (a) Relationships
   (b) Solving math problems
   (c) Making a lot of money
   (d) Staying healthy

8. Romantic empathy is having the ability to: ____
   (a) Mirror you partner's emotions
   (b) Intuit your partner's emotions
   (c) Mock your partner's emotions
   (d) Manipulate your partner's emotions

9. Romantic mind reading occurs when: ____
   (a) You can read your partner's thoughts
   (b) You are psychic
   (c) Your partner can read your thoughts and feelings
   (d) When you expect your partner to know what your thinking
      and feeling

10. Jealousy in you or your partner means: ____
    (a) You really care
    (b) You are insecure
    (c) You have good reason to be
    (d) There is something else that's actually bothering you

11. When it comes to expressing feelings in your relationship, it's
    better to: ____
    (a) Let them all hang out
    (b) Express your feelings freely
    (c) Judge each situation separately
    (d) Trust that your partner knows what you're feeling

12. Emotional infidelity occurs when: ____
    (a) You cheat on your partner
    (b) You tell your best friend everything
    (c) Your emotional life is invested outside your primary
        relationship
    (d) You lie to your partner about how you're feeling

13. One of the major signals that tells you to leave a relationship
    is: ____
    (a) You are losing yourself
    (b) Your partner is cheating
    (c) You hate his family
    (d) You are always arguing

14. You are naturally more attracted to someone who: ____
    (a) Is different from you
    (b) Reminds you of a parent
    (c) Is very much like you
    (d) Makes you laugh

15. You and your partner can use toxic or negative emotions to: ____
    (a) Create excitement
    (b) Express tensions and anxieties
    (c) Explore your fantasies
    (d) Become closer

16. Authentic sex occurs when you: ____
    (a) Are clear about what you want
    (b) Play act with your partner
    (c) Satisfy your lover
    (d) All of the above

17. The romantically intelligent approach to online intimacy is
    to: ____
    (a) Let go of all your inhibitions
    (b) Experiment with your identity
    (c) Be wary
    (d) Don't judge yourself

18. Romantic hypersight is: ____
    (a) Gazing intently into your partner's eyes
    (b) Looking closely at the character of a potential partner
    (c) Training your partner to look at you
    (d) Detecting possible flaws in your partner

19. Romantic perseverance is the ability to: ____
    (a) Get even with a lover
    (b) See your relationship through the tough parts
    (c) Sustain the passion in your relationship
    (d) Ignore your feelings in favor of what is best for the
        relationship

20. If you disagree with your partner on an important issue, you
    should: ____
    (a) Leave him or her
    (b) Try to convince him or her of your point of view
    (c) Leave it alone and live with some ambiguity
    (d) Try to compromise

Scoring:

If you got 18 to 20 answers right, you are romantically intelligent.

If you got 15 to 18 answers right, you are getting there but need to brush up on your skills.

If you scored in the 12 to15 range, you definitely need to boost your Romantic IQ.

Below 12: Don't start a new relationship until you read this book.

Correct answers:

1-b, 2-c, 3-a, 4-c, 5-b, 6-d, 7-b, 8-b, 9-d, 10-b, 11-b, 12-c, 13-a, 14-c, 15-d, 16-a, 17-c, 18-b, 19-b, 20-c.

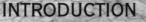

LOVE IN A BRAVE
NEW WORLD

*The only part of us that is 100 percent
honest is our emotions.*

—Anonymous

Daniel Goleman, in his groundbreaking book *Emotional Intelligence*
(1997), drew the public's attention to "emotional intelligence," or
what he called EQ, one's emotional IQ. In that book, he inventoried a
set of attitudes, personal qualities, and interpersonal skills that, once
learned, could raise millions of readers' consciousness about a previously ignored dimension of human intelligence. Goleman contends
that being "book smart" or highly intelligent in the academic sense
alone may predict how well you will solve math problems or whether
you would thrive as a professor, but it won't guarantee happiness, personal fulfillment, or worldly accomplishment. Being smart in life
requires more than a towering IQ. Your Emotional Quotient, your EQ,
is a more reliable forecaster of satisfying relationships and success in
life than your Intelligence Quotient, the traditional IQ. Your EQ is the
measure of your emotional depth and dexterity.
   Romantic Intelligence is a crash course on how to become smart
in love by applying the skills of emotional intelligence to your intimate
relationships. It may seem strange to pair the word "romantic" with
"intelligence." Yet, how many well-intentioned, highly educated people do you know who come up short when dealing with their relationships or understanding themselves? They may comprehend the nuances

of scientific theories, or string quartets, but when it comes to making their relationships work, they are whistling in the dark. They lack "romantic intelligence" or that winning combination Jane Austen (1998 [1811]) proposed nearly two centuries ago in her novel *Sense and Sensibility:* a sharp mind and a passionate nature, the two components of emotional intelligence.

Today, so much pressure is put on our relationships, there is an epidemic of "relationship burnout." Relationships get "used up" much faster than they did in previous generations, and the "rules" that govern relationships are changing faster than our ability to comprehend and adjust to them. This acceleration, plus our greater freedom to choose whom we want to be with and how we want to live, all work together to make skillful management of our relationships more complex and challenging than it used to be. In the modern world, making sense of the fluidity and turbulence so characteristic of our relationships requires a form of intelligence that includes strong social skills, self-awareness, healthy emotional self-management, and staying highly aware of your environment, in other words, living consciously.

Where can you learn these skills? Except for those who research and study behavior—psychologists, sociologists, anthropologists, motivation experts, and some philosophers—few of us learn much about how to deal with our emotions in school. No one majors in how to read someone else's feelings. There is no academic department called "Active Listening" or "Problem-Solving in Relationships." When it comes to your love life, you may get sympathy, support, and suggestions from your friends and family, but ultimately you're on your own.

When you are on your own, you might rely on Hollywood, sitcoms, or stereotyped romance-novel formulas for guidance. Or you might think you are relationship-savvy, until your partner shocks you by telling you exactly what he dislikes about you, and wonders aloud whether he should be with you at all. At that moment, your intellectual IQ crashes. You are shaken to your core and your emotional mind takes over.

Instead of absorbing the blow, processing your feelings, and figuring out what is really happening, you allow your consciousness to be hijacked by your "high-test" emotions. Strong feelings like fear, anger, physical desire, jealousy, envy, and grief triumph over your best intentions and create feelings of helplessness and powerlessness. These feelings cause you to lash out—with regrettable consequences—or to plot elaborate revenge fantasies.

When you're in love, you are particularly susceptible to losing your head and you rely mostly on your heart and erotic impulses to make crucial decisions. Mix in those potent biochemicals, your hor-

mones, provided by nature to perpetuate the human race—not to promote long-term relationships—and the likely result is romance plus
intellectual meltdown. With your mind on cruise control and your
body otherwise preoccupied, you may be smart in everything else, but
in love you act like the proverbial "fool." When you do connect with a
soul mate, what was once a promising relationship, filled with mutual
dreams and many possibilities, can fall apart fast, unless you have the
emotional know-how to make your love last.

To understand and analyze events, people, or reality intellectually, that is, with your powers of reason, is one thing. To "get it" at
the emotional or gut level is another. Your passions rule you, not your
intellect. Intense feelings like hurt, anger, jealousy, even rage, can
overwhelm you unless you understand and learn to manage the complex, hard-wired emotional circuitry within yourself.

If you've lived through one or more failed relationships, despite
your best intentions and the extra care you think you will bring to
your next romantic encounter, you are likely to spin out at the same
blind spots and to relive similar disappointments again. However, by
using the power of your romantic intelligence and developing the skills
outlined in this book, you can end this cycle of relationship déjà vu.
Brain power alone isn't enough to make you happy or to deepen (or
even sustain) your ability to stay and grow in a mutually loving relationship. You're not a creature made of logic and reason. When it
comes to your relationships, your emotions have you in their power
and actually create your "logic" and "reason."

Emotions and Passion

Love is a three-dimensional construct composed of thought, emotions,
and physical attraction. The thinking element is the aspect of love that
includes how you think about relationships in general, how you think
about yourself in relation to romance and intimacy, and what you
expect from your partner and lover. The emotional element of love is
made of how you feel about yourself and your partner; how you make
emotional connection or disconnection; your fears about relationships,
getting close, or losing someone; how jealous you are and how possessive you can become. The physical aspect includes the sexual component of the relationship, the degree of mutual affection, and the
expression of desire in an atmosphere of respect and caring.

Emotions are the bottom line in personal relationships: they light
up the electric currents that arc back and forth between two people,
and they are the keys to understanding our innermost selves. Feelings

create intensity and spawn the delirious and edgy thrills that distinguish romantic relationships from familial and friendly relationships. Ultimately, they energize and empower our dreams, embolden us to take action, and drive us to despair. Emotions shape what we see, not as observers, but as participants who feel and experience the consequences of our behavior.

Feelings fill us with the desire and the passion to undertake a quest for fulfillment, to end the tension between what we want and what we achieve. Emotions give depth and meaning to what we see and what we want. They touch us, make us laugh, and move us to tears. Emotions (if we use them intelligently) tell us what's right and what's wrong, and signal us when improvement and change are needed. Our emotions make us human.

Emotions and Rebirth

In *Romantic Intelligence,* you will discover ways to raise your Romantic IQ to become as smart in love as you are in life. Based on the breakthrough research that catapulted *Emotional Intelligence* onto the bestseller list, *Romantic Intelligence* offers an approach that blends the intensity, excitement, and passion of romantic love with emotional intelligence—a set of attitudes and behaviors that you can learn to apply to your life—to ensure that your relationship becomes the most satisfying, enriching partnership possible.

The more Romantic IQ you bring to your love life, the more meaningful and powerful your relationship will be, and the fewer the surprises, problems, and disappointments you will face. Being smart in love calls for understanding the emotional terrains and zones of intimacy—being able to identify, make sense of, accept, and manage your own emotional states in addition to understanding and empathizing with your partner's moods, feelings, and personality. Having romantic intelligence is being able to achieve the same emotional comfort level with your partner that you feel with yourself.

Understanding and altering communication skills is not always enough. Romantic intelligence requires bravery and clarity of thought and action. And though romantic intelligence is bold and fearless, it is also gentle and sensitive. It enhances honesty and authenticity and closes the gap between what you think and feel and what you say and do. When you harness the power of your romantic intelligence, you will understand more of what you and others are all about. You will feel more intensely, care more deeply, and love unconditionally.

The program we offer broadens the definition of "romance" to include the dance of self-transformation and creative synergy that evolves from conscious living and loving. We all know how fickle emotions are and how they change from moment to moment. Although such changes may be important, as a romantically intelligent person, you don't measure your love for your partner by these surface or reactive emotions, or by the inevitable disappointments, hurts, and misunderstandings that take place with your partner.

With romantic intelligence, you become more yourself, with no false pretenses, no play-acting to create good impressions for your partner. You embody the meaning and purpose of your life; you become a person of value, honor, and self-respect. Becoming emotionally honest—owning up to what you feel, not censoring or judging your feelings and emotions, will unlock powerful energies within you, and help you to better manage your feelings when you encounter the inevitable minefields of intimacy. Emotional brilliance produces honest and powerful relationships and stimulates personal growth, even rebirth.

Emotions and Dishonesty

Emotional dishonesty plays itself out on a relationship's surface, with the expression of pseudo-emotions. These are emotions that camouflage the deeper, more threatening emotions. They are "manufactured" feelings used to defend against honesty, protect the status quo, and guard against intimacy or the possibility of pain. They result in the denial of feelings, emotional numbness, or emotional withdrawal. In the chapters that follow, you'll learn to express your emotions honestly and be clearer about what you feel as well as how to avoid dishonest or inauthentic emotions. To illustrate the effects of psuedo-emotions, let's take a look at the dishonest, inauthentic couples of the type showcased in the 1999 Academy Award-winning film *American Beauty*. They were emotionally distant with each other and out of touch with themselves.

In an interview with *The Guardian* (2000) about his character Lester Burnham, actor Kevin Spacey observed, "I think Lester is very much like a lot of men in American life, who . . . suddenly realizes the lack of honesty in his life, the lack of communication—not being able to say what he actually feels and do what he actually wants. He's grappling with feelings that have long been dormant, but have been reawakened in him. It's not so much a mid-life crisis, but rather a sort of rebirth." By allowing himself to see the truth of his life and expressing what he thinks and feels, Lester comes alive and extricates himself from the suburban wasteland of the "living dead." Just before he dies, he is finally able to make some real emotional connections as he opens

real happiness of his daughter's first love and, instead
~~daughter's~~ girlfriend, he feels compassion for her and
...ner.

"Look Closer"

The sign in Lester Burnham's office in *American Beauty* reads
"Look Closer." This is to instruct himself (and all of us) to look
beneath the surface of things, past the superficiality, and see the truth
and lies of our significant relationships. To penetrate a
facade—whether it is a mask of beauty, the allure of money, power, or
a glamorous job—and see the truth under the surface is one of the
skills a romantically intelligent person has. It is perhaps the most difficult relationship skill to learn. Most of us do not have the penetrating
vision of Ricky Fitts, the young man in *American Beauty* who films his
world and exposes its pretenses, fragility, and shimmering beauty.

What does it take to create a vibrant, self-sustaining relationship
in the context of contemporary life? It starts with emotional
well-being, the ability to make a commitment to another person, and
healthy self-esteem. When things are going well for you emotionally,
you have the courage to risk getting into an upbeat and fulfilling relationship in which you are completely authentic with your partner. You
also have the understanding and emotional maturity to stay and persist
in a relationship when its luster wears off or, if it's truly bad for you,
to leave it behind you.

Jenny's Choice: A Romantically Intelligent Approach

The person with romantic intelligence has trained herself to look
closely and see the essence of someone's soul rather than the glitter of
that person's image. For example, Jenny, a musician, fell in love with
Aaron, an investor in a start-up business, whom she had met backstage
after one of her performances. Like Jenny, Aaron loved classical music
and hanging out in bookstore-coffee spots. They planned to marry and
were fairly happy together, until a weekend spent with her prospective
in-laws convinced Jenny that Aaron wasn't the right man for her.

She saw that he treated his parents harshly, and she recognized
that his overbearing attitude, particularly toward his mother, could
easily change his future behavior toward her, and become part of their
relationship. Watching Aaron interact with his mother was the culmi-
nation of many of the various unsettling incidents that she had

previously observed, but had failed to acknowledge in their relationship. His rudeness, arrogance, and insensitivity came to light when he was with his parents. Finally, all that she had refused to recognize about him became a part of her awareness.

Jenny is a secure person, self-possessed, with strong boundaries, and she has a strong sense of self-worth. She had the courage to allow her Romantic IQ to speak to her, despite the prospect of being alone again. Jenny trusted what she had seen. She also trusted her feelings and she knew it was better to end the relationship immediately than to ignore or minimize the huge problems that she was convinced would come to dominate their relationship. Even when Aaron's mother implored her not to break the engagement, explaining that her son had just sold his company for lots of money, Jenny stood her ground, never looked back, and found someone more to her liking.

Later, Jenny realized that she had fallen in love with Aaron, the image, not Aaron, the man, and she had not allowed herself to see the real person. Images are fabrications, the projection of a constructed public or social self, sometimes calculated to take advantage of (or to wow) others. Love can blind you and blur your vision so that you will form sexual bonds with a prospective mate.

We urge all lovers to enjoy the "stars in their eyes," which is the hallmark of most love affairs in their early stages. But *look closer*. Truly seeing and honestly assessing the real person you long to be with can save you from future heartbreak, and it can enhance the quality of an authentic, loving relationship. When you look closer, you make your choice secure in the knowledge that there will be very few surprises to contend with, and that your relationship is worth the problems and adjustments that will have to be faced.

The Brave New World

The times call for newer, more effective ways to manage relationships. Women and men are taking longer to commit to partnerships, establishing careers before they marry, making the choice to remain childless, having children as single parents, and living longer. All of us expect more from our relationships, but many of us are ending them sooner, with far less provocation and social stigma than ever before.

Partners are meeting through personal ads and on the Internet, conducting long-distance relationships, and dealing with long-term absences. These factors and many others contribute to an ongoing revolution in the way we conduct our intimate relationships. These changes calls for the best use of emotional intelligence with those we love and with whom we live. Because we adopt and apply the principles of Goleman's emotional intelligence and teach you how to put those principles into practice in your love life, our approach challenges many assumptions. The romantically intelligent approach supports the natural expression of all emotions as a part of relationship building and problem-solving. It does this without proposing an inborn emotional chasm between the sexes, or focusing solely on communication skills (important as they are).

Healthy expression of emotions adds closeness, richness, and passion to your love life. Like everything else in life, one's love life is an ever-changing landscape. We see the ecology of love as a delicate rainforest or Zen garden composed of various psychological and emotional terrains. Free-flowing emotions encourage flexibility in your personal relations, as well as in your relationship's ecology.

A majority of couples today live apart from their families of origin and the safety and security of a familiar community. Without these social buffers, couples may put all their "eggs" into the relationship "basket." That system can overload when emotions, expectations, and lifestyles don't fit. Couples are finding that it takes intelligence, the ability to manage their emotions, and a realistic worldview to keep their relationships healthy and alive in the new millennium.

Staying together as a happy couple also may require discarding outmoded and irrelevant beliefs about relationships. Romantic intelligence is the ability to embrace and make sense of the rapid, accelerated change that surrounds your relationship while still experiencing the primitive emotions of fear, hate, jealousy, anger, and so on.

Research shows that couples who maintain strong connections of emotional rapport, empathy, support, and shared ideas, that is, couples who have an intense friendship at the center of their relationship, promote each other's psychological well-being and potential to change and grow (Barnett and Barnett 2001). By respecting your partner's individuality and accepting and acknowledging her or his separate needs, wants, and goals, you nurture her or his natural development, a factor critically important to the vitality of your partnership.

When you are working with romantic intelligence you don't limit your beliefs about relationships. You go to the past for ideas about what makes relationships work, and you try to think about the future with insight. You do this with the goal of creating the best possible relationship for living in your environment. You reject outdated formulas that will not work, and you know that no amount of wishful thinking will bring them back. The person who has romantic intelligence knows that she and her partner do not relate to prescribed sets of rules for creating good relationships, or even what form a good relationship should take. Instead, the partners rewrite the rules to fit their continually evolving relationship, which is experienced in the present and into the future.

Optimal functioning both for individuals and relationships requires the elements of choice and passion. Choice is based on the ability to think and work through complicated issues, and then to make reasoned choices. The commitment, emotional maturity, and passion that you bring to a relationship allow you to experience and accept the entire spectrum of your human emotions. Passion informs your life with the energy for self-realization and success.

The Basics of Romantic Intelligence

To create satisfying intimate relationships you start by mastering the fundamentals of emotional intelligence. Then, you learn how to transfer the qualities of emotional intelligence into romantic intelligence. Emotional intelligence is a necessary precursor to romantic intelligence, and it is not possible to understand romantic intelligence without doing some groundwork on emotional intelligence.

It is our hope that, by the time you finish reading this book and have completed the exercises, you will be able to

* Have an open channel of awareness that enables you to recognize and identify what you are experiencing emotionally.

* Identify exactly what emotions you are experiencing in the moment.

* Assess the emotions that you're experiencing. That is, are you reacting to something that you are experiencing in the present? Are your cumulative emotions erupting after a stressful day? Has an injury, a deep hurt from your past, superimposed its memory on the present? If that is so, does that old pain erupt whenever circumstances remind you of that incident from your past? When your Romantic IQ is up and running that will help you to make sense of what you're feeling, the feeling's origins, and whether it's a ghost from the past or a present concern that is troubling you.

* Assess whether to act on your emotions or not. You will be able to think a problem through rather than acting impulsively and then regretting your action.

You will become adept at **Emotion Management,** which includes the following skills:

☆ Being able to use the strength and intensity of your powerful life-enhancing emotions to supercharge your relationships, making them deeper, more precious, and meaningful.

☆ Knowing how to push through painfully paralyzing emotions that hold you back. You will understand and accept these emotions as part of life's painful experiences, but you won't let them run your life. You will go through them and then proceed with the rest of your life.

☆ Being able to eliminate sarcasm, put-downs, needless conflicts, petty squabbles, and nitpicking as a way of saving face. You will work through an entire problem step-by-step, rather than momentarily feeling better about yourself, and "winning" a battle but wrecking your relationship.

☆ Knowing how and when to express anger assertively, not aggressively, and also knowing when not to express anger at all.

☆ Building up your tolerance for frustration and delaying gratification.

☆ Learning how to channel the energy of negative emotions into self-empowering acts. Your negative emotions can serve you rather than hurt you.

You will become proficient at **Empathy/Listening,** which means

☆ Being an open channel and tuning in to other peoples' emotional states and your own.

☆ Being able to follow someone else's emotional lead.

☆ Being able to listen attentively to what your partner is saying, rather than thinking about what you are going to say next.

☆ Being able to listen without interrupting your partner.

Finally, **Relationship Management** is the cornerstone of any successful relationship, and it is crucial to a successful union with your partner. By establishing and using the power of your romantic intelligence you will be able to

☆ Sustain your emotional self-control over intense negative emotions, so that they serve as a signal for solving difficult issues, rather than focusing the negativity on your partner to hurt, wound, and, ultimately, destroy your relationship.

✴ Be sensitive to your partner's emotional states, which will allow you to solve problems between the two of you with greater compassion. You will understand more of what your partner wants and needs from you, and you will be aware of what your partner is feeling about himself or herself, as well as what you are feeling.

Why We Wrote This Book

Our aim in this book is to move beyond cookbook formulas that may seem attractive but rarely work, and to get you to approach intimate relationships with the same passion, intelligence, and awareness that you bring to your education, career, and professional life. *Romantic Intelligence* draws on John's years of experience working with couples and individuals on relationship issues. Mary teaches a university course called "Passion and Choices" that encompasses the history, psychology, philosophy, literature, and movies that deal with romantic love in our world. We also drew on our life together, and the experiences of the generous women and men who were willing to share their stories and their secrets.

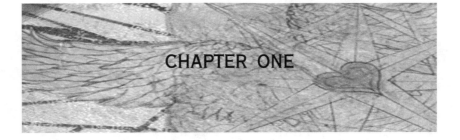

CHAPTER ONE

WHAT IS ROMANTIC INTELLIGENCE?

*Without the expression of feelings, relationships crumble, sex
becomes mechanical, giving becomes manipulation, hurts
become grudges, and love becomes loathing.*

—David Viscott
I Love You, Let's Work It Out

Most of us can become romantically intelligent. The learning curve for
improving your Romantic IQ is not very steep, because you are working with your own emotional states and with people you know very
well. In this chapter, you will become familiar with the characteristics
of the romantically intelligent woman and man. In addition, you will
determine your emotional type; that is, whether you live in your head,
cut off from your emotions; or in your heart, cut off from your intellect and only aware of your feelings; or whether you manage your
relationships with a combination of your head and your heart.

Romantic intelligence, like emotional intelligence, optimizes your
emotional mind rather than your intellectual brainpower. Being emotionally smart means you are able to pay attention to the messages
your moods and feelings send, and thus you can regulate them. You
are also fairly good at understanding the feelings and emotional
mind-sets of those closest to you.

Emotional Intelligence: The Basics

"Emotional intelligence" has become a buzzword in our culture, but do you really know what it means to be emotionally intelligent? The following basic qualities, attitudes, and skills are the bedrock of emotional intelligence. When you set out to face life's challenges, achieve your goals, and create the life and relationships you desire, having the following abilities matters more than having a Ph.D.

* You are, first and foremost, *self-aware*, which means that you are familiar with the full spectrum of your emotional states and can make sense of what you're feeling and what motivates your actions. Chapters 4 and 5 deal with the process of increasing your self-awareness and will help you to become familiar with the entire range of human emotions, including the toxic ones that many people find so hard, either to deal with or to acknowledge.

* You are capable of *empathy;* that is, you have ability to put aside your own thoughts and needs for the moment, and you can recognize and tune in to other people's emotions. You know how to listen actively.

* You are a good emotional manager. You are able to *harness and regulate your emotions*. You have the skills to turn negative feelings and emotions into energy and self-empowering actions.

* You are adept at *motivating yourself and others*. Your goal is to bring out the best in yourself and other people. That means you are spirited, passionate, able to cheerlead others and yourself.

* You are *not impulsive* and do not act out to discharge an uncomfortable feeling for instant gratification. You are able to sleep on a problem and examine it in the morning, or even at a later date. You don't need instant closure, because you can tolerate "not knowing" and you're okay with the ambiguity of waiting.

* You are generous, altruistic, and have a *positive outlook,* which doesn't mean that you don't get angry or blue, but you have the tools to work with these emotions and stay with them. You neither ignore nor deny these emotions, and you don't berate others because of them. You see your negative

feelings as beneficial messages, because you know they alert you to something important.

✶ Finally, you are *persistent*—you never give up on your dreams or yourself. You're a fighter; you know how to tough it out and you see failure as part of the process of becoming successful. You understand that failure is a part of risk-taking to achieve success, and that all successful people sometimes fail along the way.

What Makes a Romantically Intelligent Woman?

When you apply the basics of emotional intelligence to your romantic relationships, you become a romantically intelligent person. The characteristics of the romantically intelligent person apply to both sexes, but women who have high Romantic IQs have certain qualities and men have others. As you read through these characteristics, take note of what you need to work on to become more romantically intelligent.

She's a Straight-Shooter

The woman who is romantically intelligent is *emotionally straightforward*. She is aware of her emotional depths as well as the ebb and flow of all of her feelings. She doesn't try to escape her blue moods because she understands they are part of the intricate communication system within her being, and part of her network of connections with others. The way she handles and expresses her emotions is integral to the way she defines herself, as a person and in her relationships. She never plays mind games or tries to manipulate relationships by "manufacturing hurt" to make someone feel guilty. She never uses her anger to get her way.

Romantically intelligent women express their feelings appropriately. They are clear and direct in their communication; consequently, their partners know exactly where they stand. A woman with a high Romantic IQ is assertive and makes her wishes known easily. She has no secrets or skeletons in her emotional closet. She *accepts* her emotions by saying what she feels, in the moment that she feels it, but without needing to discharge her emotions haphazardly.

For example, when she's in an emotionally intense state, she would never say anything that was insulting or belittling that she would later regret. She would feel her emotions, wait until she calms down, and then discuss what's bothering her. She would not ignore or bury her emotions or allow hidden emotions to cause her to feel badly about herself. She wouldn't use her emotions to create distance with her partner, or deal with them by going on spending sprees, getting drunk, gambling, or taking drugs to counteract anger, sadness, or despair.

She doesn't judge her emotions either as "good" or "bad," but sees them as a part of her inner language. The deepest communications she has with her partner are conducted in the language of emotions. *Emotional honesty* is her most deeply held value; it is the distinguishing virtue of the romantically intelligent person.

She Is Cool and Unflappable

The woman with a high Romantic IQ has keen social skills and strong, flowing emotions that serve her well with her partner and others. She is warm, outgoing, and eager to expand her universe of friends and experiences. She knows how to deal with stress. Even in crisis situations, when everyone else around her is going crazy or acting out, she keeps a positive, can-do, calm attitude. If her mood darkens or her spirit lags, she understands why, tries to correct the problem, and when she succeeds, she changes her mood and pumps positive energy into the situation that brought her down.

During conflicts with her partner, she can put her ego and her pride on a back burner and really hear what her partner says to her, even though the message may be wrapped in an emotional firestorm. Her impulse might be to yell, scream, spew sarcasm, or shout invectives, especially if she's under attack; however, she knows how to keep her impulses in check and how to diffuse her partner's anger. She understands that the powerful, strong emotions she and her partner feel (no matter how negative or threatening they seem in the moment) pave the way for meaningful communication and fence-mending.

She Can Make a Commitment

When the romantically intelligent woman decides to make a commitment to a partner, she does it willingly and without coercion. She never commits to anyone from the position of neediness, or in the belief that her partner will be able to meet all of her emotional needs. She knows that one person can never meet all of another person's needs. She sees her partner's shortcomings as well as his strengths, but his benevolent character and good nature are the qualities she cherishes above all. Her deep appreciation for her partner and her commitment to him are reality-based, not fabricated or idealized. Her emotions are not evoked prematurely, or in momentary, passing situations.

When she makes a commitment, she know what's she's getting into, for she has thought it through and has observed her partner with his family and in a wide variety of situations. She knows, too, that she cannot meet all of her partner's needs and that her partner understands this. Although there are no guarantees, she has minimized future surprises.

She Has a Healthy Ego but Is Not Self-Involved

The woman with romantic intelligence is comfortable in her own skin. Her "self-love" and healthy ego provide her with the capacity to love her partner as he is, not as she would like him to be. Hers is a mature love that is not measured by having her needs met as a prerequisite to loving her partner. It is a selfless and generous love, without self-sacrificing behavior.

She Is Sensual and Open-Minded about Sex

The romantically intelligent woman is sexually open and uninhibited. She is open to experimentation with her partner and is clear and articulate about how she needs to have her sexual needs met. She's strongly attuned to her partner's sexual needs and, ideally, wants to create mutually empathetic lovemaking—a dance of intimacy that satisfies both partners.

She doesn't judge others' sexuality or sexual identities but concerns herself with understanding her own pleasure and her partner's. Her passionate sexuality is an expression of her strong sense of self; it is not the sole expression of her femininity nor is it used to prove her attractiveness. Her strong sexuality is a byproduct of her passionate nature. She knows that lovemaking is not always perfect and she accepts the vicissitudes of natural sexual cycles—increasing or decreasing passion and arousal—as part of the natural flow of her relationship.

What Makes a Romantically Intelligent Man?

The romantically intelligent man views his partner as well as himself as a work in progress and derives great joy from supporting and watching his partner grow, change, and achieve her dreams. Flexibility, naturalness, and spontaneity are the characteristics of their relationship. They do not cling to predefined or rigid rules about what a man and a woman in a relationship should be like. Neither do they assign stereotypical sex roles to each other. Their roles and behavior are genderless and free-floating, but, at the same time, they both appreciate their differences.

He Strives to Know Himself

The man with a high Romantic IQ has a strong sense of responsibility for his behavior; this allows him to observe himself and scrutinize his actions. He understands what he contributes to emotional situations. When a misunderstanding arises, he acknowledges that it's not just his partner's fault—he knows that he is a part of the problem. He feels secure enough in himself to see his faults, acknowledge them, and, with this understanding, he engages in successful problem-solving during relationship impasses. Integrity and honesty are the hallmarks of his style of conflict resolution with his partner and everyone else.

He Has the Courage to Face His Feelings

Self-acceptance is crucial for the romantically intelligent man. This is not to say that he will always like what he sees, but acceptance of his own human frailties allows him to work on himself to create change. As astute as he is about his shortcomings, he also clearly recognizes his strengths, abilities, and talents. He is not afraid of the new or of challenges beyond his comfort zone. In fact, in his quest for change and growth, the experience of the new is very important to him. He uses his emotions as a gauge to measure new and challenging experiences. Most importantly, he enjoys sharing his life's joys and sorrows with his partner.

He Can Commit to His Partner and to His Ideals

The man with a high Romantic IQ is genuine, authentic, and aboveboard with his partner. He can make a romantic commitment, because he lives both independently and interdependently with his partner. He has his own life, desires, and goals. He also has a shared life of mutual desires and dreams and goals with his partner. This continually shifting balance of self-reliance and dependence on his partner is the key to his sustained relationship, no matter what kind of adversity the relationship might encounter. His commitment adds meaning and purpose to his life. His relationship is not about just living to exist for another day, but about creating and sharing experiences with his partner to add joy and substance to their lives.

He Is Sympathetic and Caring

The romantically intelligent man uses his emotions to shape his decisions. Because of his emotional clarity he makes decisions that are more often right than wrong. He is sensitive to the nuances and fluctuations of his partner's emotional states because of the sensitivity and awareness he has of his own inner feelings. Romantic intelligence allows him to make sense of what he feels and enables him to assess his situation accurately, so that he manages his experiences creatively and intelligently.

Figure Out Your Emotional Type

In general, there are three basic emotional types. The first is the person who lives by her intellect or in her head. The second is the classic "emotional" type—the individual whose emotions drive her ideas and behavior. The third type is the romantically intelligent woman (or man) who, when dealing with a partner or other areas of her life, tries to balance her thoughts and feelings

Do You Live in Your Head?

Some of the brightest people with the highest IQs have some of the most dismal, unhappy love lives, or even none at all. How can this be, when they are so smart in everything else? The answer is they live in their heads, cut off from their hearts. As Daniel Goleman (1997)

put it, "academic intelligence has little to do with emotional life." It's true. Your intellectual abilities don't have much to do with your emotional mind.

Are you one of those people who pride themselves on being "rational" and "logical" in everything you do, including your relationships? Do you cherish a certain image of yourself as unflappable, unemotional, and reasonable in the way you solve problems and in your relationship? If the answer is "yes," you may be one of the Mr. Spock's of this world: those folks who conduct their relationships based primarily on intellect, not passion. Some of you "living-in-your-head" types may be driving your partners crazy with all of your logic and "sweet" reasonableness. You may even incite your partner into intense emotional exasperation because of your emotionally minimalist posture.

On the surface, you are proud to live in your head rather than your heart; you are proud not to be ruled by your emotions. But on deeper examination, you may discover that you fear your emotions and are afraid of losing control. You don't trust what you feel, and you are afraid of what your emotions might do to you and to others. You don't want to be hurt, so you refuse to engage in emotional displays. For you, feelings are messy, dangerous matters, best left to those who choose to live life with emotional turbulence.

Living in your head may give you the illusion of a greater sense of control over your life. It may seem to reduce the pain of living with hurt, disappointment, and disillusionment. In fact, many women and men who experienced troubled or difficult childhoods defend themselves from emotional pain by escaping into their books, becoming analytical geniuses, and dodging their emotions behind a barricade of theories and facts. Goleman calls these individuals "the high IQ pure type."

High IQ Pure Types

Daniel Goleman in *Emotional Intelligence* (1997) describes the work of Berkeley researcher Jack Block, who studied different emotional types and profiled their general characteristics. He gave different types separate names. For example, he described the woman who is a "high IQ pure" type as a "book-smart woman." She may project an attitude that comes off as intellectual snobbery. Capable of deconstructing a literary masterpiece, she is a brilliant public speaker, but she expresses her anger indirectly and is always at a loss for words when she needs to be honest with her partner. Characteristically, she may be prone to guilt and anxiety—symptoms of emotionally blocked minds and bodies—and she transforms her emotions into physical ailments, such as nervous twitches and tics.

Are you involved with or married to a "high IQ pure" male? This type of man has an extremely high IQ and low emotional intelligence. Generally, he is productive and ambitious, but he is cold and critical, and, as one woman who lived with this type told us, "emotionally unavailable to his partner." He is particular, hard to please, and uneasy with his sexuality or any sensual experience. He shields himself by wrapping up his emotions in arcane and pretentious language. It's difficult to know what's really going on inside him, because his emotions are hidden under a torrent of words, clever arguments, and facts.

Living in his head makes him feel superior. He may even believe that his brilliant intellectual plumage raises him above what he considers the "junk heap" of overly emotional humanity. In the story that follows, Carole is very much in love with such a man. Larry is a very smart lawyer who lives completely in his head, prides himself on his logical mind, and avoids "going off the deep end to emotional places." Carole has to decide whether to continue the relationship or break it off.

Carole and Larry: A Romantically Intelligent Choice

Carole has a college degree and sees herself as a smart woman, but after two failed marriages (she was "too young" the first time and her second husband was emotionally abusive), she sometimes wonders why she is still looking for a third husband. One day, she read the following ad in the personals column of her local newspaper:

> Extremely well-educated, very ethical, classy man, outgoing, a droll sense of humor, soaks up city life but cherishes home, hearth, and family. Distinguished in appearance, loves exercise, 45 going on 25, has room in his life for that special someone who is beautiful inside and out, height and weight must be proportionate, spiritually open.

She met Larry for drinks and they realized they had very similar "takes" on what they think is funny. They both loved to travel and had traveled widely, and they had comparable ethnic backgrounds and religious beliefs. After dating for four months, they discovered they had similar pasts and common goals. Their sex life was mutually satisfying, and they had the same ideas about family, children, and staying healthy. They seemed to be socially and mentally in sync.

Carole was madly in love and wanted to share the rest of her life with him. So Larry moved into her renovated Victorian with his teen-age daughter. It seemed as though everything was perfect. Larry was kind and playful with her eight-year-old son. They were able to talk about everything, except their relationship. Larry flatly refused to dis-cuss their relationship, or even any other problem that had elicited strong emotions from him.

"If he feels an emotion, he fights it completely," she explained. "We don't talk anything through. Instead, he sits in front of the televi-sion, and refuses to answer me." Larry's inability to take emotional risks left Carole with the sense that her deepest emotional needs were not being met and the fear that the relationship would fail. Because she was troubled by Larry's unwillingness to deal with emotional issues, his mildly sexist attitudes, and several white lies she caught him telling, Carole made an appointment with a therapist and explained that, although she loved Larry deeply, she was in a crisis about whether to continue living with him.

Her therapist told her: "Remember 'The 90/10 rule.' You can't have 100 percent in a partner. If 90 percent is great, and 10 percent is a problem, you want to think twice before you let him go." So Carole started thinking about her relationship by making lists comparing Larry's strengths and weaknesses. She discovered that his strengths greatly outweighed his weaknesses, and she became determined to per-sist in finding ways to keep her own "emotional candle lit." Larry, at Carole's request, recently has agreed to visit a relationship counselor with her to work on "Carole's problems" together.

Do You Live in Your Heart?

At the other extreme, there is the highly emotional per-son—excitable, strongly reactive, and impulsive. Are you one of these emotionally supercharged individuals? Are you unable or unwilling to control or temper your emotions? Are you intense, dramatic, and like a lot of attention? Do you crave center stage all the time? Do you emote, gush, and pour out your heart, whether you are in pain or deliriously happy and "high on life"? Perhaps you don't value your intellect, generally, and you discount its usefulness in managing your affairs.

If the description above applies to you, you prize your emotions over your thoughts. You allow your emotions to rule your perceptions rather than using your thoughts to limit the intensity of your experi-ences. If you are excessively emotional, you will lack precision and clarity in what you see and how you experience the world, because your emotions literally shape and select your perceptions. You may tend to misread or read too much into romantic situations, and you may see some matters as desperate, when they are really not all that bad. At the most extreme, the person who lives in her heart without applying her reason at all is paralyzed by reality and totally dependent on others. A hint of sadness or a disappointment sends such a person into the throes of depression. Goleman uses the word "engulfed" to describe those who are helpless in the face of their strong emotions.

Living with an emotionally oriented person can be very trying. One of the men we interviewed, Jonathan, told us that while he was walking down the aisle to greet his bride, Janice, his "heart of hearts" told him that he was making a mistake in marrying her because she is a very emotional person. Your "heart of hearts" is another way of describing your inner knowledge that is part pure feeling, part intuition, and part visionary or emotional psychic. Janice is an actress and although Jonathan dearly loved her, there had been problems even during their engagement. He had observed that she loved being the center of attention, even when she wasn't performing. She also had exaggerated little hurts and everyday problems, and she was particularly difficult when she was stressed. He suspected that the dramas she played onstage sometimes carried over into her personal life.

During their marriage, Jonathon always gave Janice the center of the stage by abdicating his own power. He indulged and fostered his wife's narcissistic needs, but could never talk to her about his feelings because she was always involved in her own emotional life. After seven years of this, they split. When you are ruled by your heart alone, there will always be times when your whole life will be thrown into disequilibrium.

Your Emotional Ecology

Barry Lopez, a well-known writer, in a recent interview talked about the nature of love as a reciprocal relationship, one that needs constant attention. He said that, "if you're continually attentive to that relationship and aware of the entropic nature of love—where through neglect it falls apart, or even with attention it falls apart—then you're dealing with something different from the common conception, that [love is] an emotion projected onto a person. . . . True love is *ecological,* in the sense that it's a complementary system, it's reciprocal. . . . (italics added) (Philippon 2002)."

Your *emotional ecology,* that is, how you feel about yourself, how effectively you deal with others, and your feelings in general, all have an impact on how well you communicate and what you say. Your emotional orientation has a tremendous effect on how well you solve relationship problems, and whether you learn from your experiences and change successfully, or you don't. Intellect alone is not enough to solve emotionally charged issues. In fact, it can get in your way. Many well-educated people understand matters intellectually and still continue making the same mistakes over and over again. As the late great comedian Gilda Radner was fond of saying, "My definition of insanity is doing the same thing the same way over and over and expecting a different result."

Daniel Goleman's and others' research into emotional intelligence stresses the central role the emotions and "the emotional mind" play in how successfully anyone manages life. The level of emotional competence or "literacy" you bring to the table determines whether your intimate relationships will be fulfilling, and whether you will do well at work.

Your emotional ecology governs the impressions you give to others and the perceptions they have of you; that is, whether they like and admire you or see you as difficult, or as a problem. Your emotions act as a filter. They affect your judgments and your view of everything; they tell you what you like and what you don't and, more importantly, whom to trust and whom to avoid. Haven't you ever felt queasy in someone's presence, without knowing why? Or picked up on someone's warmth and positive energy, without exchanging a word? Those are your emotions speaking to you and protecting your best interests. They work together with your intuition and your physical ecosystem and, if you pay attention to them, they will determine how influential and persuasive you are, as well as how much they will sway you for better or worse.

Your Emotional Mind

Your emotional mind is chronologically illogical and, like a lint catcher in a clothes dryer, it picks up bits and pieces of your past, present, and future; it holds your dreams, memories, desires, fantasies, and experiences. This part of your brain operates in the realm of what Freud called "primary process thinking." This kind of thinking has you pick the petals off a daisy to determine who your lover will be. The emotional mind, like the logic of dreams, deals with the stuff of magic, superstition, metaphor, and creativity.

Emotional Dexterity: Mastering the Flow of Your Feelings

Emotional dexterity, the ability to know, "read," and manage your emotions and those of others competently, comes from developing the *emotional mind.* Unlike the intellectual or cerebral mind where reason and logic preside, the emotional mind works instantaneously; its response time overrides rational thought because it is quicker. This "hyper" or warp speed of the emotional mind permits little or no time to elapse between the experience of an emotion and what has triggered it.

Strong, fast emotional responses can be the difference between life and death. When threatened, your response must be immediate to survive —there's no time to gather facts and make an assessment of the situation—that's the job of your rational mind. When someone cuts in front of you in traffic, your emotional mind says, "Brake!" before you think. If someone cuts ahead of you in a supermarket line, your emotional mind is immediately aware that you are being taken advantage of, and you get angry immediately. On a positive note, the same mechanisms in the emotional mind also call up the neural software that produces the romantic feelings on "some enchanted evening" when you see someone special "across a crowded room."

How to Do the Exercises

It's a good idea to buy a separate journal to do the exercises in this book. It's also a good idea to take notes on any material that seems pertinent to your situation. Do the exercises as you read. After you have read the whole book, go back and review your responses in your journal. Would you change any of your answers? Why?

EXERCISE: HOW MANY EMOTIONS CAN YOU NAME?

In this first exercise, you will look at the arc of emotional possibilities. As a human being, you have an enormous range of possible feelings. How many can you identify? Simply jot down the names of all the feelings that you can think of and see how many you can come up with. Note that generating this list will begin to put you in touch with your own emotional life.

Remember, each emotion has many tones and varieties: Anger, for example, can take the form of irritation, annoyance, hot-headedness, indignation, bellicosity, pugnaciousness, blind fury, vicious rage, and so on. The more emotions you can think about and name, the more you will become aware of the need for emotional balance, and the greater the likelihood you will learn how to live in a fine balance between your head and your heart.

Living without Romantic Intelligence

Romantic intelligence is neither emotional neediness nor a yearning for something missing within that you hope someone else can fill. Without romantic intelligence you're not honest with yourself nor particularly aware of your feelings, whether pleasant or troubling. Without Romantic IQ, you lack the courage to discuss your feelings with your partner. If that is the case, it is likely that you and your partner do not demonstrate mutual respect and support for each other, especially during difficult times.

If you are living with fear and loss, if you have shut off your feelings, or if you feel there is something missing within yourself that only the right person can satisfy, then you are living without romantic intelligence. Fears and insecurities rule your life, not possibilities. You do not know yourself completely, nor do you know what you can really do with your life. Without Romantic IQ, you do not know how dynamic and self-empowering loving relationships can be.

Romantic intelligence begins with understanding that your emotions create your reality; that they shape all of your perceptions and beliefs. Your feelings are the gateway to self-knowledge. Identifying and honoring what you experience within, being aware of all of your feelings, and knowing what they mean will allow you to take control over your life, and you will be able to move in directions that were previously blocked to you.

Holding on to Old Emotions

If you continually experience old, deep-seated, entrenched emotions, they can keep you stuck and will cut off your opportunities. If you hold on to the old, the outdated, the useless, you will stifle meaningful and fulfilling possibilities. Lack of emotional intelligence is suffocating and demoralizing. It can lead you to feel that you are inherently bad, undeserving of a better life, not entitled to healthy relationships.

Because you don't feel worthy enough for something better, you may think you don't get the breaks that others do. With your confidence and self-esteem so low, you don't expect much from yourself, or others. You feel that you don't have what it takes to succeed. What you see about yourself backs up your perceptions. But are they really true? Or is this negativity due to certain powerful emotions inside you—that have never been acknowledged by you—that may cause you to think and act in certain ways?

When you broaden your self-awareness and observe the world around yourself, you come closer to the truth of what really *is*. You stop creating a world of limitations that emanates from your pain. What you feel is what you see. Becoming truly aware of your feelings and being able to make sense of them is the beginning of experiencing romantic intelligence. When you stop limiting yourself, you stop thwarting your partner's possibilities, too. You will no longer feel threatened by your partner's individuality, independence, or different interests, because you will have your own individuality, independence, and interests.

Andrew and Jenny and Love's Ecosystem

Just before their marriage, Andrew and Jenny planted a Japanese garden behind their house to commemorate the beginning of their future and to symbolize their commitment to each other. For nine years, the garden bloomed in spring, turned brilliant colors in summer and bleak in winter, except for the red berries of the green holly. In truth, the garden did reflect the emotional highs and lows of their relationship—their moods, their periods of calm and times of storms, and the ever-changing environment of their union.

In the tenth year of their marriage, their garden had become a tangled, disorderly mass of undifferentiated vegetation. It clearly reflected the way that Jenny and Andrew were growing apart. Their sex life was nonexistent and when Andrew was home, which was rare, they argued constantly about money and how to raise their kids. In the hectic routines of married suburban life, they had lost separate pieces of themselves. When she had time to think about it, Jenny longed for the closeness of their early years.

One day they discussed the garden's decline and talked about replacing it with a tennis court. But, after some thought, they remembered why they had planted it and decided to restore it to its original beauty. They had a lot of work to do. It was smothered in weeds.

Some plants needed massive pruning, others had died from being trampled on by the children. The separate elements of the garden could not be seen, just as they had lost separate parts of themselves.

They drained the pond and filled it with fresh water and Japanese carp. Then they moved some rocks and expanded the garden's perimeters. They unclogged the Japanese maple's root system, and began to discuss the nature of the garden. Conceived of as a sacred place, remote from ordinary human experience, the Zen garden is, ideally, like love, an island of happiness—a miniature ecosystem that with proper care works, because all of its elements interact in reciprocal, mutually beneficial, and harmonious ways.

The basic elements of a Japanese garden correspond to the conceptual framework of a romantically intelligent relationship. In a Zen garden, water is always flowing. In a relationship based on the principles of romantic intelligence, emotions constantly flow back and forth between the partners. Feelings conduct the energy and information flow of the relationship.

One evening, while Jenny and Andrew were down on their knees weeding, they talked about how their marriage, like the garden, was in trouble. That was the first of many intense, deeply personal conversations. As a garden can expand its perimeters, so, too, a couple can expand their personal worlds to take in new people and experiences. Furthermore, they can feel new feelings—or old feelings that they thought they had lost forever. Empathy and mutual disclosure are the stepping-stones for increased harmony and intimacy.

♥

As partners expand and grow, their emotional ecosystem is always in a state of flux. They need to connect with outside forces, and to experience emotional shifts. It is essential for partners to stay aware of their relationship's shifting emotional terrain. Put too much pressure on one fragile spot, suppress too many negative feelings, or apply too many responsibilities to one aspect of the entire system, and the balance and order of your relationship go awry, and you or your partner will have difficulties.

If you live in a balanced emotional ecosystem, you and your partner will not be satisfied with the predictable, the ordinary, or the need for security. You will both see the worlds in and outside your relationship as places of opportunity, not sites of danger. Neither of you will stagnate because you both will always be busy learning new skills, meeting new people, exploring the new places and yourselves.

Because you don't wall yourselves off, your relationship will be in a state of constant metamorphosis—ever-changing, always evolving.

The partner you met years ago is not the same person today, and you are grateful for the changes. A relationship that isn't growing and expanding is dying. Without romantic intelligence, you won't learn that relationships are the means by which we grow and expand our being.

To be romantically intelligent is to know that your relationship by itself cannot take care of all your requirements for happiness. Thinking that it can do that places an unrealistic burden on your relationship and you and your partner will be greatly disappointed and disillusioned.

When you are romantically intelligent, you know that your partner is not "the end all and be all." Your partner can be there for you, support you when you're down, celebrate with you when you're up, inspire you to do better, and love you with all his or her heart. But it is up to you to discover your own inner happiness and your place in the world. The person with a high Romantic IQ knows that happiness and fulfillment come from within.

CHAPTER TWO

LOVE: THE EMOTIONAL COCKTAIL

*Emotions, personality, desire all spring
from flesh and chemicals.*

—Diane Ackerman
A Natural History of Love

Love: What in the world is it? An emotion? A biochemical? Is it physical? Mental? Perhaps spiritual? Is it some, all, or none of these? The word covers a multiplicity of physical sensations, strong emotions, intense desires, dreamlike fantasies, psychological leaps, sexual feelings, thoughts, and imaginative processes; it encompasses such diverse states as adoration, idealization, seduction, friendship, and even obsession.

If you sift through the works of scientists, poets, and mystics to try to understand this much-studied yet little-understood emotion, you will discover there are four basic kinds of sexual attachments that human beings make with each other that they call love: *infatuation, romantic love, intimate friendship* or *"companionate" love,* and *romantically intelligent* (or *enduring*) *love,* and there are hundreds of variations, combinations, and permutations of the four types.

This chapter looks at these basic types of love; from infatuation—the emotion that drives you crazy with desire but is likely to be nothing more than a fantasy-based obsession—to romantically intelligent or enduring love—the type of love that engages your whole self with the whole self of another—an epic saga, rather than a short story.

It is our hope that, after you read this chapter, you will be able to describe what infatuation feels like, and know how to appreciate each stage of falling in love. If we do our work well, you will understand the difference between the addictive, self-imprisoning sensations of negative excitement (this is discussed in the section on infatuation) and the self-liberating freedom of genuine love.

The Power of Romantic Passion

In legends, the power of love can turn a man or a woman into a beast or a tree, a frog into a handsome prince, and a lifeless marble statue into a flesh-and-blood woman. The power of romantic love can be miraculous, magical; it can be the ultimate transcendent form of human experience. Shaped by our earliest memories and connected to our deepest dreams, this transformative view of love is the basis of many myths and much great literature.

Romantic passion can also symbolize pain, delusion, mental illness, addiction, or a fatal attraction. This view holds that passionate love leads to self-destruction and drives us crazy. These two opposing views have dominated Western thinking about romantic love and passion since the time of the ancient Greeks. Both views acknowledge love's tremendous power, and its primary role in our existence. Few other aspects of our lives are capable of evoking such a set of powerful emotional energies and unconscious desires, and no other emotion is as complex and convoluted a mixture.

At the heart of romantic love, at its very core, our most primitive animal-based, emotional needs mix and blend with our civilized personal and cultural fantasies, and play themselves out in our attitudes about love, our choices, and our behaviors. That is why one woman we talked to described it like this, "Love is bliss and hell, hell and bliss, it's an emotional roller-coaster that's too hard to figure out, without losing your cool."

Plato thought that when humans were first created, they were one creature. In the Greek equivalent of the fall from grace they became two sexes. He said the quest for love was the search for one's missing half—and finding that missing half was the only way to be made whole.

Only love replicates the feelings of warmth and safety we felt inside our mother's body, or the safety we felt when we were held and protected in her arms. The physical closeness and emotional intimacy of love mimic that original union. To be in love and loving is the human way to transcend feeling isolated and alone in the universe.

Love enhances our self-esteem or drives it underground. Making love makes it possible for us to live in the present moment. Sometimes, love even makes time stand still.

For the most part, all human love starts with animal attraction, a purely physical experience involving all the senses, but especially taste, smell, and touch. Certain rituals, practices, and colorful displays are a part of the intimate dance of love throughout the animal kingdom. In our species, you can watch animal attraction at work wherever singles gather. Or, if you are lucky, you can observe it in your own backyard.

Each spring, we look at our backyard and watch our wild turkey flock. Mating takes place in April and early May. Wild turkeys are polygamous. The toms gobble, strut, and fan their tails, creating dramatic displays of their plumage to attract a harem of hens. At first, the hens pretend that nothing's happening, and peck away at the seeds on the ground. As his intensity and desire grows, a tom's entire head turns from white to periwinkle blue, and tail feathers spread out like a Spanish flamenco dancer's fan.

Adult males gobble loudly to attract the females, and to repel competing males. Both males and females yelp, cackle, purr, rattle, and gobble, and then disappear into the brush. The entire scene exemplifies animal attraction and basic instincts in their most expressive form.

Infatuation

According to famed anthropologist Helen Fisher (1992), over the span of four million years, the evolution of human mating practices mimicked the rituals of animal attraction; and the basic sex drive found in all animals evolved into "the human sensation of infatuation." Most likely, you have experienced this wildly passionate, intense emotional experience, perhaps more than once. Infatuation's blissful and turbulent feelings make you giddy, silly, obsessed with your lover, caught up in a whirlwind of uncontrollable urges, desires, and intense ardor. You may be going through such a rapturous phase right now. You may even believe that your intensely passionate, all-engrossing physical sensations will last, and that, this time, the dreaded cooling-off period will never arrive.

Many people believe that the strong sexual attraction and intense feelings produced in an infatuation are love, plain and simple. But animal attraction is the prelude, the appetizer, only the beginning of love's unfolding story. The sexually heightened "falling in love" stage throws your emotions into overdrive. This is nature's tactic to keep the relationship going. Once your "love chemicals" wear off, and you sober up from their intoxication, as you inevitably will, the first phase of love is at an end, and the second stage is ready to take its place, if you allow it.

In love's second, third, and fourth phases, it evolves, sometimes dissolves, and always changes, first contracting, then expanding, only to gather strength again for the rest of the marathon. Potentially, romantically intelligent love is love that goes the distance: a love strong enough for you and your partner to refine and transform yourselves and your relationship.

The Sweet Fix

You know what lovesickness feels like. There are the sleepless nights, the phone calls that you both want never to end, the chills and thrills, and the constant obsessing. You can't get him out of your mind. There's the sound of his voice that dissolves sweetly in your ear the way chocolate melts in your mouth. There's the touch of his hand that makes you feel as though your whole body is melting. You can't wait to see him; you hang on to and think about his every word; and when you do meet, you're both on love "speed," and you tremble. You don't need food or sleep; you feel giddy and light-headed, satiated, and every minute feels like you just won the jackpot—the emotional lottery.

Erica and Chris

When Erica recalls her first days with Chris, she remembers them this way: "I felt really floaty, out of touch with reality." She has chosen to spend her life with Chris. They have been together for eight months and just signed a lease on an apartment together. "We were e-mailing each other almost constantly," said Chris. "Just being away from her for a few days made me realize how much I wanted to be with her—and that was after only fifteen days. I remember that was the first time we were separated for an entire day, ever since we began seeing each other."

Chris and Erica are experiencing infatuation, the type of love that produces physical symptoms, much as an illness does, although you're not really sick. Infatuations like these can completely blot out family, friends, and coworkers, who may be alternately bemused and annoyed by your mutual absorption in each other and your obliviousness to anyone or anything outside your romance. Psychologist Dorothy Tennov interviewed and tested hundreds of individuals and couples, and documented what she found in *Love and Limerence*

(1979). She describes the common symptoms of infatuation, which she calls the state of "limerence," this way:

★ The most common emotional and physical sensations are excitation with increased heart rate and pulse, a heightened sense of aliveness, a preoccupation with thinking and fantasizing about the person you're in love with, and moments of ecstasy.

★ You devote your time and energy to the "love dance" of your courtship and divert your attention from all other pursuits.

★ If you feel that the relationship is not moving fast enough, or that your partner is cooling off, you may experience the dark and terrible feelings of fear, despair, depression, anger, and jealousy—the double-edged sword of the romantic phase of your relationship.

Lovesickness

Infatuation can occur at any time, from childhood into ripe old age. An intense passion-based emotion, it is also called lovesickness, "limerence," or obsession. Characteristically, it is a relationship in which you and your lover have limited knowledge of one another. Infatuation involves your fantasies and projections; your lover reflects your secret yearnings and desires. In general, these yearnings are unrealistic and idealize the one you desire. The infatuation can persist just as long as your idealized picture is not marred by the reality of getting to know the person you're mad about. That is, it persists so long as there is no real interaction between the two of you. While you are infatuated, there is hardly any communication between the two of you. This silence allows you to create your ideal mate in your mind.

Infatuated love is like a cocktail in that it mixes with other emotions to produce one intense, undiluted, powerful emotion. As Elaine Hatfield and Richard Rapson (1993) explain, love "cross-magnifies" with other primary emotions like fear, anger, joy, and sadness, to produce dizzying and profound effects. Passionate love or infatuation is experienced as a rapturous physical sensation. But it's also psychological—a dramatic mind/body event. Infatuation certainly causes a biochemical explosion. It ignites the desire to be swept up and carried away from the predictable, ordinary boredom of everyday life. It is a test-tube full of liquid emotions, infusing your mind and body with adrenaline highs, endorphins, and other chemicals with long names—a potent cocktail that kicks in when you're yearning to bond with someone.

Psychologists Hatfield and Rapson (1993) have argued that infatuated romantic passion may be even more intense and electrifying when amplified and fed by the other emotional combinations it blends with, such as jealousy and ecstasy, insecurity and fear of abandonment. In other words, both pleasure and pain fuel your infatuated passions and produce the highs associated with the experience.

EXERCISE: How Familiar Are You with Infatuation?

How many times have you experienced the soaring highs and weighty letdowns of infatuation? Do your relationships ever move beyond this emotional roller-coaster phase? Read the following list and check off the symptoms of infatuation you have experienced. In your journal, note how often you have been through this phase of love, and think about whether you were truly in love at the time.

_____ You felt a passionate desire and intense longing to be with the person you were infatuated with.

_____ You felt a deep yearning for your feelings to be returned by that person.

_____ You experienced the "bliss and hell" syndrome, or mood swings, depending on how the person you were infatuated with responded.

_____ You had flamboyant daydreams about that person.

_____ You lived in constant fear of abandonment and rejection by that person.

_____ You were hypersensitivite to that person's responses.

_____ You felt a deprived when you were away from that person, as if you had a "hungry heart."

_____ You felt as if you were floating on air when that person had positive responses to you.

_____ You felt obsessive and you had intrusive, constant thoughts about that person.

_____ Your felt incomplete and lonely when that person was far from you.

_____ You ached to be with that person all the time.

_____ You felt a constant need for that person to reassure you.

_____ You concentrated your whole focus on that person, and changed your life to accommodate him or her.

If you checked *any* of these sensations and behaviors, then you have been infatuated, and you know what it feels like. The more items you checked on this list, the more addicted to infatuation you were or still may be. And if you are *still* addicted to what infatuation feels like, the more you will require these kinds of feelings in any future relationship.

We call infatuation the "supernova" in the galaxy of love, because its life span is so short and its passion so intense that it can't sustain itself, and burns quickly. Michael Liebowitz of the New York State Psychiatric Institute has studied the brain chemistry of lovers; his research backs up the reality of infatuation's short shelf life (1993). According to these studies, infatuation produces certain biochemicals that act as natural amphetamines. They flood our emotional core, which is found in the limbic system of the brain, and make us feel spacey and optimistic, giddy, and euphoric. Apparently, the same "upper" is also present in chocolate. That's why we crave that sweet pick-me-up.

Love Junkies

Infatuation can strike without warning at any time and place. It knows no age limits (although it is experienced more frequently by younger people), and it has little regard for time, setting, or marriage vows. Infatuations are fluid, start quickly, and have abrupt endings. Infatuations begin affairs. They are the sudden, powerful attractions of adolescents toward teachers of either sex, movie stars, and famous personalities. Infatuation is the addictive love Madame Bovary sought with a succession of partners, all of whom disillusioned her, and the highly charged dangerous liaisons seen every day on TV soap operas.

This short life span is the reason some people turn into love junkies. When the biochemical love high wears off, they crave another fix, so they leap into in another relationship, and then another, and another. . . . Infatuation loses its potency in romantic love after one to three years; then, a couple either moves into a less intense phase of love or breaks up. In fact, researchers (Liebowitz and Klein 1992) who used other chemicals to block the so-called love chemicals found that love junkies, without their "drugs" do make long-term commitments and become satisfied with more supportive, less intense relationships

Stuck in Infatuation

As the intensity of infatuation fades, the "fever" breaks; your emotions become diluted and lose the intensity, excitement, and allure of infatuation. You may feel you have fallen out of love. In fact, when you experience this shift, you are moving into love's next phase, the uncharted territory of fear and surprises, complete with new sets of problems and options. You may fail to see this dilution as the beginning of a new phase in the evolution of your relationship, but give it a chance. When you are stuck at the launching-pad stage and expect the rockets to perpetually fire themselves, you go from one relationship to another, always seeking the intensity of the blast-off. But the fireworks never last, while the disappointments and relationship disillusionments pile up.

Some people are more susceptible to staying stuck in the infatuation phase of love. They never move off that platform to the less intense but deeper intimacy that characterizes romantic love. Those who have intense fears of loss and separation, who are insecure and dependent, who suffer from low self-esteem or are very needy, are particularly vulnerable to the passions of infatuations. All of their relationships fall apart because they are built on the fantasies and projections of the lovers, images that have little relation to the real individuals.

When you feel insecure, unlovable, worthless, and self-hating, you avoid your self. You block your own access to your *self-love,* that natural self-esteem and self-respect that point you toward fulfilling your potential and expanding your abilities. The more you circumvent your unexplored and rejected self-love, the more you project it onto someone else—an unobtainable lover or, if obtainable, someone not suited to be your partner.

The Hook of Negative Excitement

Possibly, you thrive on infatuation's "negative excitement"—the thrill of not knowing where you stand—the suspicion that your lover is seeing someone else besides you, or the despair of unrequited love. Infatuation means having a relationship with someone when you are afraid of intimacy. It may involve love triangles, it may be more situational, i.e., triggered by what is happening in the moment, and also can be ignited by loneliness or boredom, when the object of your infatuation fills a void rather than adding an element to your already satisfying life. When reality sets in, and you discover that the person you're infatuated with is only human, infatuation disappears quickly. Then, you may feel angry at the person you were infatuated with, because he or she failed to live up to your fantasies.

Few are immune to experiencing the intensity of an infatuation. However, those with romantic intelligence rarely mistake infatuation for the mature and enduring love they seek, or have, with their partner.

Romantic Love

Romantic love may begin with infatuation. But either it ends after the infatuation phase or it evolves into a more complete friendship-based love where lovers connect emotionally, physically, and spiritually. Romantic love also can begin with a friendship that smolders for a long time and then suddenly turns into passion.

Romantic love is similar to infatuation because it too is based on idealization of another person and on the romanticization of the emotion of love itself. Nevertheless, because romantic love is based on a real lover rather than a fantasy or idealized person, it is a step closer toward total commitment; it includes more of the real personalities and less emotional angst in the relationship. Many couples describe the sensation of romantic love as feeling like "we can talk about anything for hours" or "we just have a great time laughing and doing things together."

After its initial stage passes, romantic love is a less intense emotional experience than infatuation. It could be called the comfort food of love. The high-comfort levels the partners share, the tenderness, intimate bonding, and trust allowing for emotional disclosure, all induce feelings of commitment, deep attachment, and willingness to be emotionally open and vulnerable to the partner.

Romantic relationships may involve many kinds of love at different times, but each type derives from the attachments we made in childhood with our parents. The Russian novelist Leo Tolstoy understood romantic love's multiple dimensions. His epic novel of tragic and happy loves, *Anna Karenina,* depicts both the tempestuous, adulterous passion of Anna and Vronsky that ends in despair and death, and the warm, compelling bond that builds between Kitty and Levin who say their love is firmly rooted in their souls.

Falling in Love: The Progression of Romantic Passion

Four years before she walked into a friend's living room and fell in love at first sight, an astrologer told Karen not to worry about finding new love after her divorce. She said that Karen was fated to meet "the love of her life" in about four years. After her divorce Karen dated several men, until one winter evening, three months before the four-year interval was over, she attended a dinner party at a friend's home. She was seated beside the man destined to become her life partner, and, in an instant, Karen knew that he was the one. All her pre-existing fantasies of the perfect lover had become flesh. He embodied everything she had ever longed for in a partner. His build and looks, his interests and intelligence, his values and approach to life, all matched her conscious and subconscious desires.

Although rare, love at first sight is possible—even a reality—for the lucky few. For most women and men, though, falling in love is a process that begins with the senses—sight, smell, taste, touch—and quickly turns into various imaginative behaviors. The French novelist Stendhal was one of the most astute observers of the process of falling in love (1822). Even today, psychologists and theorists about love rely on his observations and cite the seven-stage process he described of how our emotions work when we fall in love. We don't have the space to discuss all seven stages, but the first three stages are of interest and are worth examining here.

Stage One: Early Stirrings

When you begin to fall in love, you admire the person and start to feel he or she is special. You marvel at the way her hair glistens, or you think his smile is sexy, or you remember with pleasure the way he spoke to you. You start to dwell on his special qualities; thoughts about her intrude into your consciousness. He stirs and touches you. Anticipation follows. Your fantasy machine revs up as you start to imagine whether this person could feel something for you, and you wonder what he or she thinks about the stock market, or that new CD you just heard.

Writer/director Nora Ephron understands this first stage of falling in love perfectly. In films like *When Harry Met Sally, Sleepless in Seattle,* and *You've Got Mail,* she excels at depicting romantic love's "warm and fuzzy" first stage. That precedes the next stage when you hope that this relationship will really take off, and there are strong indications that getting together is a real possibility. At that point, your fantasies about commitment and the future start revving up. Unlike the early stirrings of romantic love, when thoughts of the special person occupied 10 percent of your time, in stage two, you fixate on him or her about 80 percent of the day.

Stage Two: Crystallization and Idealization

Crystallization and idealization are two of the most interesting operations in the process of falling in love. Both operations take place early. *Idealization,* or total blindness to a lover's flaws, is common both in infatuations and love that turns into obsession—the lover is not loved for who he or she is, but is loved as an idealized object. *Crystallization,* a term first coined by the novelist Stendhal and later adapted by Tennov, is "that process by which an ordinary person becomes transformed in the mind of the lover into glittering perfection" (1988).

A fairytale like *Cinderella* makes this miracle of romantic love's transformation take place instantaneously, when a girl in rags is transformed into a glass-slippered princess. The creation of a real life princess or prince develops over time. Three things happen to you during the crystallization process: you think your lover is perfect; you fantasize being loved by this splendid person; and, simultaneously, you experience the awful fear that it won't ever happen. During this phase of falling in love, your main goal is to merge totally with your lover, to fuse your souls and identities into one new and beautiful entity, and to obtain an emotional commitment from your lover that he or she will always love you.

As you can see, falling in love is a totally subjective, even artistic, experience, a collaboration between your imagination and your emotions that can transform a normal, run-of-the mill person into a god or goddess, for at least two to six months. You create and color the one you love from the palettes of your childhood, your internalized images of the ideal lover, and your fantasies. Others may not see what you see. You are the artist who creates the illusion of this perfect person based on your notions of what an ideal lover should look like and be like.

What's also interesting about crystallization is that you may see the flaws and shortcomings of this person, but unlike idealization, where you don't see the flaws at all, you turn them into positive attributes. In other words, you may consciously rationalize his moodiness as being "highly sensitive." Her bad temper may translate into being "a woman full of passionate intensity." We believe that this kind of emotional rationalization, or denial, during crystallization is a necessary component for securing the love bond, just so long as you know what's going on.

Stage Three: Sustaining the Illusion

Romantic love is similar to infatuation because idealization is present in both of these aspects of love. In romantic love, the person who has won your affection is known, but still idealized. For many people, the thrill and intensity of romantic love in the beginning is such a strong aphrodisiac that to prolong the high of romantic love they must ignore or misread their partner's qualities. Anything less ruins their *illusion* of romantic love.

When both partners are on their very best behavior, that is called the "courtship" phase. This temporary, somewhat artificial experience has the purpose of sustaining and prolonging romantic intensity as long as possible. Until this phase plays itself out, the routine and ordinary experiences of daily life don't interfere with the illusion, because romantic love is a relationship constructed almost entirely of pure emotion and behavior calculated to impress and elicit admiration.

The important thing to note here is that when you fall in love, you are falling in love with an image or an illusion of someone whom you have rendered "perfect." Falling in love dumbs you down and, in many cases, blinds you to the practical, unromantic aspects of your relationship. That fact creates both the immense joy of falling in love and the disillusionment that ends in heartbreak. Shakespeare understood this dynamic very well and made fun of it in many of his plays, but most especially in *A Midsummer Night's Dream* where Queen Titania, in the throes of love's illusions, falls in love with the actor named Bottom who wears the masked head of an ass during most of the play.

Companionate Love

Many social scientists have used the label "companionate love" (also called friendship or married love) to refer to an affectionate bond based on warmth, shared values, habits, and familiarity. Sternberg and Barnes define companionate love as "a long-term committed friendship, the kind that frequently occurs in marriages in which the physical attraction (as a major source of passion) has waned" (1988, p. 89). This kind of love is what we probably wanted our parents to have (love without sex) or the style of love that we might have envied in a neighboring family.

Companionate love is not a stage of falling in love but rather the end product of some romantic relationships, the kind of love that evolves when romantic lovers have been together for a long time. The partners tend to be the best of friends but not necessarily the best lovers; there is intimacy and familiarity without passionate intensity. Not all romantic love becomes friendship, and not all friendships turn into romantic love. Some married lovers are content with companionate love, others grow discontented and seek romance outside of their commitment, or they leave the marriage and start a new relationship. Ann, one of the women we talked with, had a happy twelve-year companionate marriage with Dan until he died. She regrets that after his death she was swept away by an infatuation.

Dan and Ann

Ann, who is in her early forties, earns her living as a secretary in a small college in Plattsburgh, New York. She is both a widow and a divorcée. Her marriage to Dan ended in grief when he died of brain cancer. Looking back now, she says that, although Dan was not an accomplished lover and had little interest in sex even in their early years, he had been her best friend, her supporter, and her intimate confidante; he was a partner whose values and goals made an exact match with hers.

While she was still grieving Dan's death, she met Ed. He was charming, and their sexual encounters were always thrilling. Unlike the easy give-and-take she had known with Dan, she became consumed by passion when she was with Ed. Then they married, and she got to really know him. In just three years, he spent her entire inheritance from Dan. She lost her house and ended up in bankruptcy court. She had not recognized that Ed had a problem with alcohol. Nor had she known that he made a habit of preying on grieving widows. Her love life devolved from a satisfying, comfortable marriage to a nightmare that left her embarrassed, impoverished, and enraged. One year later, divorced and living with her parents, Ann is just beginning to rebuild her life.

Often, a woman may have a few infatuations and then find a more stable, mutually satisfying partnership. Ann was unlucky because she was susceptible, lonely, and vulnerable. She learned far too late that the man she trusted was exploiting her emotionally and financially. Today, Ann is the first to admit that she should have "looked closer" and checked into Ed's history. There were clues that she recognizes now, but chose not to see at the time. The next time she becomes involved with someone, Ann will be much better prepared to be romantically intelligent.

Romantically Intelligent (or Enduring) Love

Romantically intelligent love is a continuing passionate involvement that brings out the best in you and your partner. It allows room for both of you to grow, expand, and give each other emotional support. This kind of love allows for the self-discovery that changes you both for the better. It improves and builds your character. It challenges you both to face your flaws and shortcomings, while you strive to strengthen your bond of love and heighten your passion for life with each other.

An enduring relationship, or complete love, evolves from romantic love. These are loves that are like still rivers that run deep, not the turbulent, shallow rapids of infatuation. Enduring loves "incorporate or draw on more aspects of the self than any other kind of love—our sense of life, our sexuality, our body . . . our self-concept, the cardinal values that energize our existence," writes psychologist Nathaniel Branden (1997, p. 37). This kind of connection with someone you love, trust, and share your life with is a way of coming home to your essential being.

When you experience the complete love of romantic intelligence, it doesn't feel like an emotional cocktail, because your feelings are not based on idealization, fantasy, or projection. You love your partner simply because of who and what he or she is—your love for him brings you joy in his successes, elicits your support when he falters, and causes you to fully accept his humanity, even when he is at his worst. Your love is deep, imperturbable, with few seismic shifts. This doesn't mean that it's boring. Like a charcoal ember at the bottom of a barbecue pit that smolders after the guests have left and the kitchen's been cleaned up, your capacity for passion stays alive, and your sexual desire doesn't die just because the heat of courtship is over.

Romantically intelligent love doesn't mean that you won't have disagreements. Instead, you agree to disagree in the spirit of the freedom and honesty that characterizes your relationship. You may still find some of your partner's habits objectionable, but you learn to live with some of them, and you work on some of the others together. You have habits that annoy your partner, too, and you know it.

You are both romantically intelligent enough to know which issues are so important that you will both work on them to create change, and which issues you can both learn to live with. You discover you can't change everything about your partner to suit yourself, as you realize that your partner can't change everything about you to suit himself or herself. Nevertheless, you have the love, commitment, caring, and support of your partner because the two of you are dedicated to loving each other for who you are and who you are becoming.

Romantically intelligent love fulfills the panoply of human needs, longings, and desires. It allows us to express our emotional intelligence in dynamic and self-empowering ways. There are some couples who stay deeply in love for many years. Their love changes over time and becomes more resonant, less selfish, and more generous. The partners are one another's emotional support system and clearing house for new ideas and projects. Their romantically intelligent love allows them to share pain and pleasure, values, children, pets, secrets, and a common history filled with laughter and intimacy. Their love endures in spite of any hardships or tribulations.

The Benefits of Romantically Intelligent Love

Enduring love has many benefits. It makes you visible, even special and important, because someone else recognizes your unique talents. Love allows you to get in touch with your deepest emotions and passions, to become emotionally naked and vulnerable. It gives shape and meaning to your life. But, most importantly, when you achieve complete romantic love, it is the care, support, and cultivation of *your partner's* abilities, talents, and opportunities that provide you with the greatest sense of satisfaction.

Love has the power to give you the courage, strength, and endurance to face yourself. It can even mean giving up the image you've might have created of yourself, a false image of who you think you are. Sometimes you will find that your lover is the antidote to the imaginary, inauthentic self you may have created, someone who always brings you back to your original state, the essence of your humanity. The emotional props that you may have constructed for yourself crumble and collapse in the presence of enduring love.

Your Partner Is Your Mirror

With romantic intelligence you become aware that your partner is the mirror that reflects your hopes, dreams, and flaws. In other words, your partner's issues reflect your own unfulfilled desires. Has your partner disappointed you? Yes, when you disappoint yourself. Do you find at times that your lover is moody or uncaring and preoccupied with himself? Yes, because his moodiness mirrors your mood swings. His less-than-caring attitude and his preoccupation with himself, as much as you might hate to admit it, are like mirror images of your own insensitivities. That's why you get so upset, so disappointed, and feel so let down by your partner. Your partner reminds you about the parts of yourself that you would rather forget; the petty, selfish, hurtful, and irresponsible aspects of yourself. These mirrorlike reflections are what make love such a test. Who wants to be reminded of those parts of ourselves that make us seem utterly unlovable?

Your Partner Is Your Life Coach

The other side of love is so strong, powerful, and meaningful that some of us are willing to face our illusions and break through them despite the pain of doing so. In enduring or mature love, we find a love beyond sensations, beyond self-interest. In enduring love, we find the relationship that allows us to realize our destiny as human beings. When you lack the faith in yourself to grow, mature, and express your creativity, your partner will see your potential and coax forth the abilities you have that you cannot see in yourself.

The partner who shares your complete love and is your life coach expresses your own self-love and caring by means of his or her behavior. Such a partner supports you in reclaiming and owning those wonderful qualities you see in him or her, that you have projected onto him or her. Your partner respects your virtues, is sensitive to your moods, feelings, and needs, and loves you unconditionally because of the sum total of all your strengths and weaknesses—all the qualities that make you uniquely you. To love unconditionally does not mean you share all of the same ideas, or that you adore every aspect of each other, rather you love despite and because of your differences.

For the romantically intelligent person, understanding the emotion and the reality of romantic love allows some measure of control and reason while in the grip of powerful feelings. The person with a high Romantic IQ uses this phase of romantic love to examine the relationship and see whether a potential life partner is suitable, rather than rushing blindly into a commitment that could end in disillusionment and pain. From such a beginning a complete, enduring love can develop.

CHAPTER THREE

YOUR ROMANTIC
LIFE STORY

*I never feel that I know people well without knowing
something of the narrative of their loves. . . .*

—Ethel Person, M.D.
Dreams of Love and Fateful Encounters

The novelist Tom Robbins once wrote: "It's never too late to have a
happy childhood." He was right. Did you know that romantic love is a
powerful way to compensate for, revise, and resolve many childhood
hurts, and thus rewrite a happy ending to your life? To write that
happy ending, however, you must first come to a deeper understanding of your story; you must examine your personal romantic history in
a systematic, critical way. Most people won't look back at their lives in
this way unless they're in therapy or writing a novel or screenplay. But
retracing your love life and reviewing your patterns, repetitions, satisfying relationships—and big mistakes—are essential steps toward
becoming more romantically intelligent.

Your Emotional Package

When you meet a partner, you don't bring just yourself to the meeting.
You carry along with yourself an *emotional package,* that is, an enormous

set of internal networks composed of neurons and neurotransmitters, genetic combinations, personal memories, childhood experiences, multitudes of mental images, emotional models, and your "love map," an invisible, subconscious protocol that governs what turns you on and what turns you off.

So does your partner. The emotional content in both packages is hard-wired and complex, hard to untangle, and a hodgepodge of buried feelings, individual expectations, and interpretations about love and life. No wonder that mixing and blending these two packages together to make one relationship is hard work.

Your Emotional "Spin" on Life

Most of us can recall our childhood joys and pains, the roster of our past loves and friendships, our favorite films and love songs, and the combined mixture of voices, images, memories, and fantasies that, unconsciously, determines the people we choose to fall in love with and the relationships we choose to have. Your emotions determine how you interpret your life stories to yourself, and the stories you tell yourself continue to affect and change your emotions. There is a continuous feedback loop.

Because of the ongoing interplay between your emotions and the events in your life, your memories are interpretations of what you experience. For example, sometimes your mother might have raised her voice with you when you were a child. Her harsh, "Don't play with your food—just eat it!" signaled her disapproval and potential punishment if you didn't do as you were told.

If she had just been instructing you in table manners, her harshness might have left a simple memory of the instruction; but if she also criticized you, and called you "bad," and made her love for you provisional, based on whether you did what were told to do, you also learned that love and approval might be conditional. Then, if and when you remember your mother's harshness when she said, "Don't play with your food—just eat it!" you might interpret your memory as just one more unhappy instance of your mother trying to control your life.

The Partner Pleaser

This pattern of reprimand and approval, the memory that love can be given and quickly taken away, can produce the specific anxiety of being abandoned, disapproved of, or rejected. If this was a consistent pattern of your caregivers (mother, father, or other adults responsible for your welfare when you were a child), then you would have learned to see their disapproval as catastrophic and you might have developed a pattern of "people pleasing" that lasted well into your adult years. You may believe that people pleasing protects you from the anxiety of being abandoned or rejected.

People pleasing may protect you from anxiety, but it also does a great job of protecting you from the truth of your own feelings. If you continually try to please your partner or other significant and important people in your life, you are not able to experience the full interplay of emotions with them, or the inevitable contradictions, disagreements, and conflicts that are important parts of truthfully engaging with your partner and others. Instead, you try to appease, so that no one might get angry with you. You don't make your wishes known for fear of disapproval. To feel safe, secure, accepted, and loved, you may subvert your needs and think only of your partner's.

If you are a partner pleaser, you never disagree or say "no" to your partner, even when you secretly want to. You may even lose touch with what you really want. When you measure your partner's behavior as "all or nothing at all," that is, as either totally accepting you, or totally rejecting you—with nothing in between—then the rich complexity of your relationship disappears. Your interpretation of your relationship with your partner and the uncomfortable feelings that result from your interpretations of your partner's feelings, motives, and behavior may all be filtered through your childhood memories of conditional love, and those filters may be obscuring your vision.

Your Emotional Defenses and Signals

In addition to your interpretations of your experiences, your defenses create distance from difficult events and painful relationships. They repress certain emotionally unpleasant memories, and color the "spin" you give to your emotional life. *Spin* is the angle from which you see things, the attitude you choose to adopt. You can choose to be open about what you feel and comfortable with your feelings, or you can ignore and deny them.

Having romantic intelligence means not only are you in tune with every emotion you feel, you can also make sense of your feelings. Most importantly, you accept the experience of actually feeling, in your body, every one of your emotions as an integral part yourself. The more open and accepting you are of your emotions, the more honest and interesting you become as a person. Furthermore, when you understand and accept what you feel, the more sensitive you become to what others feel.

You don't have to *like* feeling the negative, uncomfortable, or threatening emotions. No one *likes* feeling jealousy, rage, or grief. But you do have to honor them when you feel them. That means you have to be aware of what you feel, when you feel it, and the way that you do that is by naming what you feel to yourself and not trying to hide from it. Being romantically intelligent means that you trust your emotions enough to recognize they provide a clear, direct signal when something is wrong and must be addressed. Your emotions and their accompanying physical sensations tell you to move toward someone or something, or to move away.

When things are right between you and your partner, your emotions also let you know that—loud and clear. The more positive and joyous emotions you share with your partner, the closer together you will grow.

Your Genetic Makeup

Your personality and temperament, how sociable you are, how you process emotions, and how you actually manage emotions are all affected by genetic predispositions that you inherited. Were you a cranky, calm, or fussy baby? Infants demonstrate different temperaments almost from the minute they arrive. Some babies are born whiners and cry a lot; others seldom even whimper; some infants are timid, fragile, and sensitive to everything going on around them; others are alert, interested in everything they see, and almost aggressive in the way they cry to be fed.

So, initially, you are predisposed toward having a particular temperament. But because you're human and possess built-in flexibility and enormous potential to grow and change, your environment and the impact of your ongoing experiences will change and modify your genetic predispositions.

In other words, although your genetic makeup may point you in a certain direction, your personality and temperament are not fixed, immutable characteristics like the color of your eyes. Your human capacity to change and the strength of your natural resiliency make you unique. They can help you to rise above the most oppressive, even tragic, circumstances, to realize and express all of your human potential. They can help you to develop your romantic intelligence, even when that may seem to be an impossible task.

Your Romantic Memoir

Ask any friend and, most times, he or she will be delighted to tell you their love stories. Your friend Rob remembers Laura, the bridesmaid who caught his sister's wedding bouquet; when they kissed in the coatroom, she smelled of soap; she promised to call him in a week but never did. You probably remember your first crush—the lifeguard at the pool one summer, the sixth-grade teacher who made you blush, the movie star who sent you an autograph.

Each of us has a set of private memories that, when looked at chronologically, add up to a romantic memoir. This memoir would include your early and "insignificant" associations, your first kiss, your first sexual encounter, your wedding night, or three, four, or more significant relationships, losses, hurts; everything you can remember about your love life, how you felt about it then, and how you feel about it now.

Writing such a memoir is one giant step you can take to improve your Romantic IQ. Note that as you try to remember details from your memories, it is quite likely you will experience a series of deeply felt emotions and sensations. If that happens, stay with what you feel in the moment you feel it, for as long as the emotion lasts. If it overwhelms you, let it. It will pass. Then when it has passed, write about the experience of feeling that emotion. It may prove to be very helpful for raising your Romantic IQ.

The process of mapping your romantic history begins by first thinking about your memories from early childhood to the present. Then, in your journal or on your computer, write down what you remember of your romantic memories. You can do this exercise in the form of a timeline or as separate entries, depending on which form is more comfortable for you. The exercise may take several weeks or even months to complete, depending on how much you choose to write. It gives you permission to think about and assess every detail of every romantic encounter you ever had.

Writing your personal love history will open up important emotional doors within you to reveal your deepest feelings. Taking such an inventory of where you've been, where you are now, and where you are heading is liberating, and ultimately it will empower you to move on to a richer and more fulfilling period in your life.

Writing your love history may release buried memories you hid from yourself years ago. Writing your personal memoir also may serve as a trigger for a dramatic release of feelings you chose not to deal with years ago, and have been ignoring ever since—feelings that have held you back from expressing your romantic intelligence.

EXERCISE: Writing Your Romantic Memoir

As you write your romantic history, look for any patterns that seem to repeat themselves. For example, is there a pattern of having feelings for and intense connections with people who aren't good for you? You might recognize that you have been attracted to certain kinds of toxic people over and over again, perhaps people who are controlling, distant, competitive, or very different from you in outlook, interests, and personality. Also look for healthy, life-affirming patterns in your romantic history. Make two lists. One of the relationships that were good for you, the other of relationships that were not good for you. List as many individuals and incidents you can remember, in as much detail as you can remember, and assess their impacts on you.

These details are important because they will put you in touch with your hidden feelings. When you are as honest and open with yourself as you can be, you will discover new insights about yourself and your relationships. While you write, be sure to describe the feelings that accompany each entry. The most important part of this exercise is to stay open to your own memories. Do not censor your thoughts or writing. Free-associate. Don't be afraid to include the sexual details. To help you get started, here are some questions you might want to answer in writing:

♥ Are you still angry with a past lover? Is it hard to let those feelings go? If it is, why do you think this is so? What would happen if you did let that relationship go and moved on with your life?

♥ Do you miss having sex with a former partner, although you know he or she wasn't an emotional match for you?

♥ Watch and observe how your relationships have changed or are changing. Pick up on the patterns. Think about the important relationships you have now. How do they make you feel? What about your partner? How does he or she make you feel?

♥ Write down the qualities that make your present relationship so special. What do you think needs to be improved? Why? How do you think things would change for you and your partner if more of your relationship issues were solved? Where do you see your relationship one year from now; five years from now; ten or more years from now? Do you feel happier, stronger, more productive and more confident now—or did you feel more self-empowered, fulfilled, and happier before you entered this relationship?

♥ What were the circumstances that created this relationship? How did you feel about yourself at the time? What did your parents or others do or say that significantly influenced you about relationships, love, and how you feel about yourself? What have you done to make things better or worse for yourself through the years, and why?

These are some of the questions that you should ask yourself while you write your romantic memoir. The more you can remember to write about, the more helpful this exercise will be to you for gaining a greater understanding of your own romantic past. That, in turn, will affect your ability to create romantically intelligent relationships in the present.

The Romantic Cover-Up

Notice, too, the "spin" or explanation you give each story from your past. When you've been hurt, or spurned by someone you loved, you might protect yourself from further humiliation and pain by creating stories about human nature, or by telling yourself, "that's what people really are like." For example, many women who have had a series of bad experiences with men generalize from their experiences and say, "You can't trust any men."

When people are hurt, they tend to generalize rather than personalize their experiences. This type of story—or spin—is a way of avoiding becoming intimate again, and a self-protective myth to insulate the speaker from further emotional pain. We call this kind of storytelling "The Romantic Cover-Up." When you produce a personal narrative that whitewashes your experiences to erase the pain, you are engaging in a romantic cover-up. Observe and become aware of the kinds of stories you tell to yourself.

Your Emotional Memory Bank

A separate part of your brain stores your emotional experiences and all the memories associated with them. You can think of this neural-electronic network as a warehouse or as a memory bank full of various emotional wounds, traumas, frightening, or painful incidents, as well as happy and joyful experiences. Some of your memories will be more emotionally charged than others. Like streaks of lightning in the thick, heavy air before a storm, they may reignite and produce currents of supercharged feelings.

Other memories will be vague, dim, and not as emotionally strong; their impact on your present-day feelings is minimal to nonexistent. All of your memories serve as a template for organizing and keeping alive your emotions from your past. All that is needed is a present-day experience with someone somewhere to spark a stored emotion, pleasant or unpleasant. A current situation may trigger an intense but distant memory and recreate or reignite past emotions.

That's why sometimes you don't understand why something or someone bugs you so much, especially when you know the situation shouldn't really bother you. An old memory may flare up causing you to feel anger or pain. The next time this happens, remember, you may be hitting a tender area in your emotional memory bank.

Repressed Emotional Memories

Your emotions also determine how you *feel* about what you remember. When you're on emotional overload and the intensity of what you feel is uncomfortable and frightening, the natural tendency is to repudiate or disclaim those sensations and memories, and to somehow get rid of those intensely distressing feelings. *Repression,* the unconscious act of burying what you feel, is a defensive psychological operation. It works by pushing your emotions so deeply down into your psyche that they become imprisoned in the emotional equivalent of solitary confinement. The memory of those feelings becomes buried inside your heart and soul. Such repressed, impacted emotions are forgotten by your conscious mind, but they still have an effect on your life. They can become a psychic burden that literally weighs you down.

Repressed emotions can cause emotionally erratic behavior and they can even generate symptoms of physical illness.

Emotionally Charged Memories

Perhaps sometimes you are baffled by what you feel, and you don't understand why you're so angry or depressed. As stated above, there are times when your emotional reactions have nothing to do with your present-day circumstances, but they have been triggered by events or people around you that blow out fuses from your past. Consider the following story. It illustrates this point.

Lonnie and Jim

Lonnie and Jim were daily running partners. One morning Jim called Lonnie to tell her she would have to find another running partner that day because he was called away on a business appointment. Lonnie instantly became infuriated and she yelled at him before hanging up on him. After she hung up, she wondered why his bowing out for one day had caused her to become so enraged? She knew she had overreacted, so she thought about it, and suddenly realized that Jim's innocent behavior reminded her of her ex-husband who had refused to run with her at all, because she was "too slow." Recognizing that her emotional past had fused with her present circumstances, she called Jim back, apologized for raging at him, and rescued their friendship.

Everyone has occasions when they react to other people and events not as they are now, but as they were in the past. For example, suppose your father humiliated you in front of your friends when you were a teenager by always calling you "skinny bones." Today, when your lover pays you a compliment about how good you are looking, if he even touches on any aspect of your thinness, you might go ballistic.

To be romantically intelligent is to be able to understand your emotional sensitivities, to name or label what you're feeling, and then to reflect on the origins of your emotions. Ask yourself, "Am I really reacting to my partner or the situation in the present? Or is it past pain that is causing me to react so strongly now?" Overreacting to slights or snubs, real or imagined, is usually the tip-off that stored painful emotions from your past have been reactivated.

Think about what pushes your emotional buttons. What gets you going? If you are highly sensitive about particular issues like your weight, height, speech, temper, values, lifestyle, the job you have, educational attainment, and so on, it is quite likely that there is an emotional thicket from your past surrounding the issue. It is an issue that you have not yet faced nor healed. Clearly, you still have work to do on the pain that you experience around those sensitive issues.

Discover Your Hidden Love Map

Many of love's projections and identifications happen outside of your awareness and understanding. Nevertheless, they shape how you relate to others emotionally. *Projection* occurs when you mentally throw, or project, your ideas and difficult emotions (such as pain and anger) onto another person as a defense against your own anxiety. Then, you can react to those emotions through that other person. *Identification* occurs when you copy and mirror the feelings of another person. You make them your own. That is, you begin to think, act, and feel like that person through a psychological identification.

These covert psychological operations may begin at an early age. You may not know it, but, according to Helen Fisher (1992), by the time you are about eight years old, you have created what sexologist John Money calls a "love map," etched deep in your unconscious mind. A love map is an internal geography or *subliminal template* of what turns you off, and what turns you on.

What this means is that years before you became intrigued by that certain smile of your lover's, his laugh, her brains, or his charisma, your brain circuitry was already receptive to certain cues and images, sounds, and situations. Why? Because memories, images, film clips of family and friends, movies, TV ads and visuals, plus chance associations all come together to form an unconscious blueprint or configuration in your mind, to produce the patterns of your love map. Your love map is particular to both your individual history and your cultural background.

For example, there is a notorious love map described by Sigmund Freud in his account of the "Wolf Man." (The patient was called the "Wolf Man" because he was obsessed with a character in a fairy tale.) In Freud's brilliant but frequently disputed interpretation, he retraced the many complex twists of his patient's difficult love life (1971). The patient, an aristocratic but neurotic young man from Eastern Europe had come for treatment because he was troubled about being able to enjoy sex only in one particular position.

After deep analysis, Freud determined that when the young man was a child, he had first seen his mother, and later on their serving maid, kneeling over a bucket scrubbing the floor on her knees. Apparently, the child found the posture very erotic. So, by age five, he had configured and mapped a powerful part of his unconscious love map. Consequently, as an adult he was able to achieve sexual satisfaction only if his partner duplicated those specific postures that had cast such an erotic spell on him as a child.

EXERCISE: DISCOVER YOUR HOT BUTTONS

Your personal love map colors and explains why you fall in love with one person instead of another, and it has an effect on what arouses you, sexually and emotionally. Now, in your journal make a list of at least ten of your personal turn-ons. Then add ten or more of your personal turnoffs. List physical attributes and character traits that you find either irresistible or unappealing in a partner. Do you like dark hair or blond? Does a mustache turn you on or off? Some women prefer men who are bold; others prefer very hairy ones. Some women like very talkative men. Others are turned on by the strong, silent type. Just make two lists of what appeals to you and what doesn't. After you've made the lists, study them for a while.

As you will see, your subconscious mind has amassed quite a few bits and pieces of traits and characteristics that appeal to you. Were you aware of your preferences before? Bringing them into the open may help to explain certain of your behaviors and help you to distinguish your deeply etched likes and dislikes from the qualities and assets of a romantically intelligent partner.

Another dimension of your love map might show you that you seek a partner who embodies the qualities you desire for yourself, an *ego ideal*. What you find most attractive in a partner might be that part of yourself that remains buried and unacknowledged. For example, Ellie was always falling in love with actors, although she herself was too shy to speak in public. She watched her partner from the audience, sitting in a back row of the theater, and never realized that her own deepest, most secret wish was to be an actress.

The deeper you can delve into your fantasy life, the more intelligent and informed you will become about who you are. The more you know about yourself, the less you will need to filter your perceptions through a prism of distortions that mask the reality of your relationships. Achieving greater clarity about the meaning of your past and present behavior will empower you to change your life for the better.

Your Parents' Bond

How can you dig more deeply into your subconscious mind? You can begin by examining your parents' relationship or that of other caregivers who were a significant part of your life in your childhood and adolescence. The way the relationships in your family of origin were conducted taught you their rules on how to act, feel, and think about the significant people in your life. Your original family created your emotional blueprint of who you are, how you should act and feel, what you should do, and what you should avoid doing.

EXERCISE: Discover Your Emotional Blueprint

Use the following questions to think about how your parents solved problems, disagreements, and misunderstandings in their relationship. Use the questions as a guide to discover how your parents laid the foundation for how you think and behave in your relationships today. Write your answers to these questions in your journal.

1. Did your parents talk with each other, or did they talk at each other? Did they listen to each other? Did they try to make changes to improve their relationship?

2. Did your parents constantly bicker about irritations and issues that they never seemed to be able to straighten out? Did they sulk?

3. Were there tension-filled silences and withdrawals by one or both of them when they were angry with each other?

4. If one of your parents withdrew from the other, was it your mother or father? Who was the pursuer and insisted on talking? Who was the distancer? Who would withdraw into silence?

5. What were your parent's notions of what a relationship should be?

6. What did they tell you about adult relationships?

7. What did you observe about adult relationships?

8. Did your parents have a traditional relationship with strict rules about gender roles? Or were they nontraditional, sharing tasks and roles without regard for gender?

9. What did your parents appear to expect from each other?

10. How much closeness or distance did you see your parents have with each other ?

11. How did your parents handle their conflicts? Did they get angry with each other? How did they show their anger?

12. Did your parents show their affection with each other openly? Or was it rare for them to show signs of intimacy and affection? Perhaps you never saw your parents openly expressing affection with each other. Was this the case?

13. How did your parents order their priorities among their selves, marriage, children, and work? How did you know about their priorities?

Now, on a new page in your journal, make lists to answer the following questions:

♥ What emotions were encouraged in your childhood?

♥ What emotions were allowed to be expressed in your household?

♥ What emotions were not allowed?

♥ What emotions were not recognized or ever addressed?

♥ What emotions were labeled "bad"?

Now, as best you can remember, think long and hard about whether there were any traumas in your parents' relationship. Major relationship traumas include the discovery of extramarital affairs, unresolved grief, and psychological or medical problems. If there were such traumas, think about how they affected you. If your parents were separated or got divorced, think about what impact those events had on you and your feelings about relationships. Think back and try to remember all the lessons that you learned about men and women from your parents. Then write several paragraphs in your journal about your answers to these questions.

In most cases, your parents taught you something about sex and intimate relationships. Or did they hand you a book and expect you to learn all there was to know about love and sex from the printed page? Perhaps they expected you to learn these matters from your peers or health classes. If there was open discussion about sex and marriage in your household, what impact did those discussions have on the way you conduct your relationships today?

Becoming aware of your romantic past includes assessing your parents' relationships, and their influence on you as models. Your parents' bond in the past is a key to understanding how you relate to and behave with your partner in the present.

Love and Rebellion

Because it crosses social class lines, ethnic backgrounds, and religious and racial affiliations, romantic love is sometimes put to the test by having to overcome obstacles, usually of a social nature, like the disapproval of parents or friends. The plot of every romantic novel follows the familiar scenario in which two lovers meet, fall in love, overcome many obstacles, and finally get together happily at the end. In novels, overcoming social restraints and barriers proves how deeply two people truly love each other. This scenario is so popular in our society that many lovers look for obstacles to overcome and exaggerate their "us-versus-them" mentality.

With romantic love, these dynamics usually originate in adolescence when teenagers are trying to establish their independence from their parents. By disobeying their parents' wishes and society's dictates, they try to establish their independence and individuality. Rebellion is a common motivation for falling in love but only rarely does it have the staying power that love rooted in mutual respect and admiration has. In the next chapter, you will discover how getting to know yourself better and learning to understand your true motivations will encourage the growth of a higher Romantic IQ.

CHAPTER FOUR

EMOTIONAL SELF-AWARENESS: THE KEY TO ROMANTIC INTELLIGENCE

Emotion is the chief source of all becoming conscious. There can be no transforming of. . . . apathy into movement without emotion.

—Carl Jung,
Psychological Aspects of the Modern Archetype

What makes for the best possible relationship you can have with yourself and your partner? What allows true intimacy to flourish, and happiness and contentment to be the rule, not the exception? What sustains your love life through the best and worst of times? The answer is romantic intelligence, and the key to your romantic intelligence is *emotional self-awareness,* the ability to be in tune with and understand your feelings, even if they change from moment to moment.

In truth, how rocky or smooth your relationship is depends on the strength of your emotional self-awareness, and how tuned in you are to your emotional ecology. Recall the discussion in chapter 1 about emotional ecology. There, we said that emotional ecology is composed of many complementary elements, including how you feel about yourself, how effectively you deal with others, and your feelings in general.

Your emotional ecology regulates your actions and reactions, your thoughts and feelings about yourself and those around you.

The internal environment within you is the total of all your experiences and all that you are. Possessing emotional self-awareness allows you to be clear about what you feel when you feel it. It also allows you to accept your feelings, whatever they are, and not judge yourself for feeling any emotion, whatever that might be. When you feel anger, you know you are angry, and you accept the truth of your anger. If you feel emotional pain, you acknowledge that you are hurting. Emotional self-awareness makes you more real, honest, and authentic with others, and with yourself. It enriches your relationships as it improves and deepens your own experience of life.

The first step to being able to regulate your feelings and work with your inner ecology is to be able to identify and name your moods and emotions. At the center of the world within your being you will discover your wise, intuitive inner voice, which will provide you with the truth about the complexities of your emotional experiences.

Imagine Your Inner World

Emotional self-awareness involves becoming familiar with a strange land within yourself: the green valleys, snowy peaks, dark caverns, and hidden grottoes that make up your inner landscape. Childhood memories reside there, in close proximity to secret dreams. Old hurts and new ones mingle and blend. Your hopes for your future mix it up with the lyrics of your favorite song. When you visit that landscape for the first time, it may seem very strange, but, to become romantically intelligent, you need to visit it frequently, and you need to become familiar with its inhabitants and landmarks.

Most of us experience our feelings with varying intensity. Some of us are more excitable than others; some deny or ignore the strength of their feelings some of the time; and still others demonstrate very little emotional intensity no matter what the situation warrants. Karla McLaren (2001) put it this way: "It's hard to find that middle ground in our emotional landscape."

Many people have difficulty experiencing their emotions, that is, they don't know what they are feeling *when* they feel it. They may be cut off from what they feel; or they may be ignoring and denying their own bodily sensations and emotions. Often, such people allow their friends, family, experts, and cultural norms to dictate to them which emotions they should feel, under which specific circumstances. Or they must be told what they should feel, *when they don't really want to know*. They stay "ignorant" to preserve their self-esteem rather than come to grips with the true impact that they have on others. They repress their feelings.

Repression is an emotional delaying tactic. It tamps down a feeling and sends it to your unconscious. The feeling disappears from self-awareness and goes underground, where it's out of sight but not out of mind. Repressing an emotion is the most familiar and well-known form of emotional defense. It is the opposite of emotional expression or the acting out of emotions.

The Landscape of Your Emotional World

How would you describe your inner world in ecological terms? Do you imagine it as a lush rainforest where everything is in balance and the ecological relationships are in equilibrium? Do you see a sandy desert where trees and feelings are scarce? Or do you see a mudflat flooded with rain? Some of us feel our emotions so intensely that our inner life is like a water world drenched by sporadic downpours and monsoon rains. Other people are so emotionally parched they feel very little of what goes on inside themselves; they live in a metaphorical desert cut off from the restorative waters of emotional healing.

EXERCISE: DESCRIBE YOUR EMOTIONAL LANDSCAPE

Sometimes it's easier to "see" your emotions by creating a picture of what you think they look like, instead of trying either to feel them, or to make sense of what you feel. In your journal, write a paragraph describing your inner ecology, the terrain where your emotions reside. Try to visualize your inner landscape. Describe the plant life and atmosphere; think about the creatures that live there.

After writing your description, ask yourself, "What am I feeling, right now? Am I depressed? Anxious? Content? Happy?" Remember, you can feel only one emotion at a time, even though you may think your feelings overlap. You may feel contradictory emotions, but when people say they're confused, it's a defense against what they're feeling. Emotions are layered but you can be aware of only one layer at a time, starting at the surface and working down to the deeper emotions. For example, being angry usually indicates underlying pain.

There can be a rapid cycling of emotions but it's still one emotion at a time. Can you laugh and cry at the same time? Can you feel happy and sad simultaneously? Of course not. To make sense of your love life, you need to be deeply aware of what you feel, especially at those times when you cycle through a series of strong, contradictory emotions very quickly. Eventually, you will be able to sort out the contradictions, if you are aware of them. You need to "own" every emotion that you feel.

Emotions Drive Actions

Feelings are so powerful they can cause you to break into song on a wet, miserable day or send you back to bed on a sunny morning to spend the day under the covers. All of your choices—deciding what you want, how you want to spend your time, and where you want to be—come about from your feelings. "Your feelings may be exaggerated, distorted, displaced, confused, or overstated, but they are your feelings," says David Viscott (1987).

Knowing your propensities to exaggerate, project, dramatize, or underplay your feelings can clue you in to your true motivations. For example, if you habitually exaggerate, that means you want to prove something. If you always underplay your feelings, that means you are uncomfortable with them, perhaps worried about them, maybe even afraid of them. If you dramatize everything you say, that means you want to be noticed or applauded. If you project your feelings, you may be doing that to see what is really going on within yourself. When you understand what you are *doing* with your feelings, then you will have a better understanding of why people treat you as they do.

For example, "road rage" is the common expression used to describe a driver in the throes of a strong emotion with the propensity to exaggerate his or her feelings. That person sitting on your tail, honking before the light turns green, cutting in and out between the lanes on the freeway is, most likely, expressing inner emotional turmoil. He spews anger on the anonymous drivers as opposed to attacking the people who cause his anger. The other drivers, the objects of his anger, are not real to him, so he feels it's okay to take out his rage on nameless others. The road "rager" turns his outer world into a reflection of his inner world. She sees other people as obstructing and slowing her down, causing her to feel powerless and helpless. Her animal (*limbic*) brain takes over her forebrain, and her emotions take control of her driving, which then becomes extremely dangerous.

People with high Romantic IQs understand that emotions like rage are much more powerful than mere thoughts. When was the last time you were motivated by your thoughts? Emotions can make you passionate about an idea; they can embolden you to win a tennis match, or inspire you to start a family. Your emotions are the power source behind your thoughts; they determine what you choose to think about, choose to do or not do, whom you commit to in a relationship, and whether you stay committed. Your thoughts work in sync with your emotional reactions and assess the information you have stored in your mind from your experiences. Yet those experiences were stored in your memory largely based on what you felt about them.

Self-awareness is a significant component of romantic intelligence. By *self-awareness* we mean your ability recognize what you experience emotionally from moment to moment. To be self-aware is not to deny, ignore, displace, or repress your emotions. Emotional self-awareness is essential to psychological well-being and physical health because it provides the foundation for the choices you make and the directions you take. Everything that you do from buying new shoes, to getting a new job, from going back to school, to committing to a partner or ending a relationship, all these acts originate in your emotions.

Romantically intelligent relationships are awash with feelings flowing with emotional intensity and passion, but they are not flooded by them. That's because feelings flow freely between the partners, but they are never overwhelmed or flooded with negativity or toxicity (Goleman 1997).

Your emotions are not who you are; they are only what you feel at any given moment. They are your teachers and spirit guides, the guardians of your boundaries, the gatekeepers of your integrity, and the conduits of information from the inner sanctum of your essential being. Emotions are neither good nor bad. They are an aspect of your humanity. They are the complement and soul mate of your thinking brain.

Emotions Are an Issue for Us

It used to be thought that men were not as emotional as women, but the truth is that men and women are equally emotional. Men may tend to repress their feelings because of cultural and gender stereotypes, but they are less inhibited about expressing their anger than women are. However, most men are more inhibited about expressing their emotional pain than most women are. This is not to say that most women express themselves freely. Many women are still uncomfortable with expressing their thoughts and feelings in a straightforward way. They still find it difficult to locate the emotional middle ground between keeping the peace at all costs, and the intense expression of very intense feelings.

Despite the media image of Americans as very open and friendly, Europeans and South Americans, as a rule, are less reserved about expressing anger, joy, fear, even grief, without feeling ashamed, shy, or "on stage." Emotional styles and expression do vary from country to country and culture to culture. We know that our emotions are exploited and manipulated by the media (especially fear). We also know that the expression of emotions in sports events, both on and off the playing field, is one of the few avenues of emotional expression that is socially approved for men. Think about the way that football players can grieve like children when they lose, and how they exult and hug each other when they win.

In the United States, it seems that only during times of national trauma or tragedy do we feel free to express our heartfelt emotions without feeling painfully self-conscious. The tragedy on September Eleventh culminated in a national outpouring of emotions that fueled our courage, hope, and patriotism. The nation's emotional defenses collapsed with the buildings that day as, collectively, we coursed through an entire spectrum of emotions—intense anxiety, panic, depression, despair, outrage, fear, and terror, and powerful life-affirming emotions such as admiration for the heroes, empathy and pity for the survivors and their losses, and love for our dear ones.

Why are our emotions so difficult and frightening? Why do so many of us fear expressing our feelings, even pleasurable ones? One reason they may frighten us is that they can seem endless or boundless; they can't be measured like a cup of flour or a dozen eggs. Another reason we fear emotions is they can make us feel out of control. They seem to come from out of the blue. They can sneak up on you without any warning, and before you know it, you're sobbing uncontrollably or erupting with anger. If you aren't aware of how you are feeling, an experience like that can be very scary.

The invisible landscape inside you produces physical and psychological sensations, flare-ups, and feelings of loss or exclusion that are hard to identify, much less resolve. You can even experience difficulty with joyous, uplifting emotions because they, too, can cause you to feel uncomfortable, especially if you think that you don't deserve happiness, that you should feel guilty, or that you deserve to suffer.

Knowing Who You Are

Self-awareness requires having a "self" that feels and loves and knows itself. Being able to sense your inner core and becoming familiar with your emotional nature provide you with knowledge of, and access to, your self, the whole person you are—in essence, your being and identity. Your self is that the fixed part of you that remains unchangeable through time.

When you claim that you don't know who you are and complain that you feel empty within, then self-awareness and the ability to express romantic intelligence are elusive, nearly nonexistent possibilities. When you are strongly self-aware and have a powerful sense of a self, one who grows and evolves throughout your life, then romantic intelligence is a real possibility for which to strive.

To have a strong sense of self is to be honest and authentic with others, yourself, and the world around you. You don't pretend, you don't playact, you just are. This very powerful and attractive state of being energizes and boosts your romantic intelligence and brings new meaning to your experience of love and passion.

To be self-aware is also to be independent. It's always easier to conform than it is to be independent. True independence requires inner strength to deal with criticism and disapproval. When you are independent, you are anchored to and propelled by your inner beliefs, rather than tied to the beliefs of others. Only when you are true to yourself, can you can be true to others.

Your self-awareness also includes a fundamental awareness of others' feelings and motives. To be self-aware is to have the ability to determine whether others are caring and generous or self-serving and selfish. To be romantically intelligent is to have the ability to read others clearly, to look beyond someone's surface and really see what's going on in that person's heart.

Romantic intelligence requires you to be open to the inner experience of your feelings and thoughts without censoring them. When you are romantically intelligent, you can grapple with distressing perceptions and feelings because they do not threaten who you are. Instead you know that your perceptions and feelings reflect your humanity, empathy, and compassion, in addition to informing you about your anger, resentments, and hurt.

Your emotions rise to the surface because of your thoughts, your dreams, others' remarks, external stimuli like art, music, and nature, reminiscences about the past, and speculations about the future. Emotions are either pleasurable or painful and, like people, they have distinct characteristics; they come in different shapes and colors, even sounds.

According to David Viscott (1987), the "name given to an emotion depends on when the feeling occurs." For example, *anxiety* is the fear that you will experience pain in the future; *hurt* is experiencing pain in the present; and *anger* is frequently a response to pain in the past. Anger occurs only after you've been hurt in the immediate present. In this chapter, we will deal with anxiety and hurt. Chapter 5 discusses anger.

Anxiety: The Fear of the Future

Anxiety is the fear of being hurt in the future: the anticipation of pain, distress, or loss—not now, but later. Anxiety looks ahead to an unpredictable and ambiguous future—concerns that, in themselves, lead to further unremitting worries and anxiety. Anxiety surfaces when you think about the possible loss of love; for example, you may worry that your lover will abandon you for someone else, especially if there are problems in your relationship, and you're not sure where it is going. Anxiety provokes you to imagine scenarios where your lover abandons you.

Anxiety, more than most emotions, has an acute physical dimension. This very physical experience may involve rapid heartbeat, sweating, palpitations, dizziness, upset stomach, nausea, emotional dread, fear, and even panic attacks. It also has a mental component: catastrophic thoughts can hijack your mind with the notion that the absolutely worst thing in the world is about to happen to you, your partner, and your relationship.

Anxiety is a very tricky emotion because it can be based either on an imagined possible outcome, or a real fear. For example, if your lover betrayed you in the past, and you don't trust him in the present, you may be anxious that he will betray you again in the future. This type of anxiety derives from hurt you suffered in the past, rather than from hurt in your present reality, but it can torment you nonetheless.

From time to time, a certain amount of anxiety can be a close ally; it can put you on "yellow alert" to watch for impending danger. Have you ever been out with someone who evoked mild anxiety in you? You couldn't put your finger on it, but there was just something about that person that made you uneasy, guarded, uncomfortable. Pay attention to such feelings. It is quite likely that your intuition picked up on the person's negative energy or you sensed the person had the potential to be a troublemaker.

The function that anxiety serves is to warn you of possible danger. Anxiety is exquisitely sensitive. Feeling some degree of anxiety releases just enough adrenaline to add to your mental sharpness when you are working on a task or have to make a speech or give a presentation. Anxiety is like emotional radar; when used well, it can be your ally.

However, when anxiety becomes an intense, chronic state, it takes on a life of its own, and you can't control it. It cuts you off from the freedom to experience life the way you want to and eliminates your ability to act spontaneously. In extreme cases, anxiety can reach panic levels or cause you to experience pains in your chest and make you think you are dying.

EXERCISE: DESCRIBE YOUR MOST ANXIOUS MOMENTS

Think of a situation that makes you feel anxious. Is it when you have to speak in public? Public speaking is the Number One fear; for many people it even outranks the fear of death. Does your anxiety peak when you ask your boss for a raise, or when you make a demand on your partner? Does intimacy put you on edge, making you feel vulnerable and exposed, ripe for fresh hurts? Do you get extremely nervous and self-conscious when you grow close to someone?

In your journal, make a list of at least five situations that provoke anxiety in you. Do these situations cluster around relationship issues, such as the loss of love, the fear of abandonment, anger, or conflict? Are they connected with financial concerns or issues of security? Do health issues provoke your anxieties? Perhaps you fear growing older or losing your looks?

Identifying the areas that trigger your anxieties will make you more aware of the issues that need your attention. For instance, if issues about speaking up for yourself in a relationship terrify you, you will need to discuss these matters with your partner; or if you are alone, you might want to talk with a therapist or other counselor about why closeness or asserting yourself is so frightening. The first step in dealing with fear is being honest with yourself about what the fear is about. Once you assess your particular problem area, you can figure out your options for remedying the situation. Options can range from informal discussions to formal therapy, drug therapy, couples therapy, hypnosis, or any combination of these.

Hurt

Hurt is pain and distress in the present. Hurt is reddish purple, the color of wounds. Hurt is the kind of pain that sizzles and burns your heart as if you were a toddler who injured her finger pushing a bobby pin into an electric socket. Hurt announces an injury and informs you that you're in pain. Hurt sets limits and breaks your spirit. Hurt can be activated by the less-than-delighted look on your partner's face after you have had your hair done a new way and worn a new outfit for a special occasion. Your feelings are hurt. If you don't express the fact that you're hurt—"Ouch that smarts!"—you are likely to feel that hurt over and over again.

If you expect your partner never to hurt you or let you down, you are thinking unrealistically, and that kind of thinking can pollute the emotional flow of your relationship. For instance, suppose you are playing golf with your partner and you make a spectacular putt for a birdie. "That's nice," is all your partner says while concentrating on his own line. You might be hurt that he didn't make more of your success. You might feel that he hadn't praised you enough.

But if you were a romantically intelligent woman, you would also ask yourself, "Where is this hurt coming from? What is enough praise, and where is my need for praise coming from? Is this old stuff?" You would also try to understand that your partner wants to make his putt, too. You would chalk it up to human nature and not carry your snit with you to the next tee. Thinking in absolutes like, "He will never hurt me," is simply asking for trouble.

Love Hurts

Love always hurts. No matter how good the relationship is, no matter how long love lasts, love always hurts because we are human and don't live forever. Love also hurts if a lover abandons, betrays, or exploits you. The only way to eliminate hurt and heartache from your life is to hold yourself back and never allow yourself to love anyone. If you don't risk the hurt, you can never know love; you remove yourself from what Nathaniel Hawthorne (1959) called "the magnetic chain of humanity." The human chain Hawthorne refers to is the never-ending circle of love and hurt and pain and hate and human connection. Hurt comes with love's territory.

Do You Turn Your Feelings into Symptoms?

Ever since the late nineteenth century when hypnotists and early psychotherapists discovered that sexually repressed women could convert their emotions into physical symptoms like hysterical blindness and uterine pain, psychological therapy has focused on blocked emotion as the root cause of many physiological illnesses. Some of our most common expressions, e.g., "You're a pain in the neck (or the butt)" come from this human predilection for displacing, blocking, incorporating, and literalizing emotional distress into a physical symptom. The process is called *somatizing,* which is where the word "psychosomatic" comes from. An emotion like anxiety can hide for years before it emerges as a physical symptom, especially in cases of sexual molestation or other types of physical and psychological abuse.

Some people are so sensitive to their emotional environment they will pick up on any tension in a room and turn it into a sinus headache. Another person will get extremely angry and have a coughing fit instead of dealing with her rage. Some people are emotionally porous. That is, they are psychically susceptible to the emotional atmosphere. For example, if they are in a place where people are sad, they become depressed. Their emotional boundaries are porous and fuse with the prevailing emotional climate, whether it is a holiday party or a tense meeting.

If your emotional radar is extraordinarily keen and you are prone to picking up on others' emotional states, it's important for you, as best you can, to surround yourself with positive people and supportive environments that nurture your emotional health, not "vampirize" it. Emotional vampires, those people who drain your emotional strength and prey on your life force, are particularly hazardous to your well-being.

The Journey to Emotional Self-Awareness

Learning to become self-aware isn't easy; it takes patience and persistence. It is difficult to alter the way you see the world and yourself. To see things differently is to rewrite the story of your life or, more precisely, it is to change the interpretation of your life that until now made sense to you. When you become more emotionally self-aware, you will see things differently. Sometimes you will view your relationships and yourself in a harsh glaring light and sometimes in soft focus, but, regardless of the quality of the light, when you are more self-aware, you will see matters differently.

Always Pay Close Attention to Your Feelings

Self-awareness starts with attentiveness to your own feelings. Paying attention to what you are feeling is not just a matter of *saying* what you feel because verbalizing only "intellectualizes" your emotions. Self-awareness is experiencing your emotions in your body, in the moment, in the here and now. Whether the emotions are comfortable or uncomfortable, you do not deny, ignore, displace, or repress what you feel. You are totally connected to all the faint clues, blaring sensations, and visceral nuances of all of your feelings.

To live only in your head, because you are uncomfortable with what you feel, or because you do not trust your emotions and you are afraid of losing control, guarantees a lousy connection with your partner and with the other significant people in your life. To guard and protect yourself from what you feel is the equivalent of wrapping yourself up in a cocoon and dehumanizing your relationships. Living only in your mind results in the loss of vitality, meaning, and passion. Living only in your mind is the difference between actually experiencing life and reading about it, as if life were a novel to be read instead of a life to be lived.

What are you feeling right now? Are you calm? The way you might feel floating on your back in a lake, watching the clouds go by? Are you tense or twitchy, as if a mosquito were buzzing in the room, and you can't see it, but you know it will bite you the minute you aren't looking for it? Are you feeling sad, left out, or just in a bad mood, and you don't know why? Is anger flaring in the little nerves around your neck?

It is important to monitor what you're feeling moment by moment, as consistently as you possibly can. At first, this may seem very hard to do. New and different behaviors are always hard at first. It also may be tiring to sustain because making a strong conscious effort to really feel your feelings moment by moment can be tiring. With practice, however, it gets easier and eventually it will become second nature to you.

Exercise Emotional Impulse Control

When you *think before you act* on your emotions, you are exercising emotional impulse control. It sounds simple, but sometimes it is difficult. You simply allow yourself to feel whatever emotion you may be feeling, while you consider how you are going to express your thoughts about that feeling. Or, you may decide not to discuss the matter at all. It might be counterproductive. You might even want to wait and cool down before discussing it, you have that option.

When you don't exercise emotional impulse control, you may satisfy a momentary urge to vent or to release tension, but you cannot see things in new and different ways and you cannot solve problems. Slow down. Step back. Anxiety and fear-based solutions lead only to greater confusion and turmoil. Slow down and look for guidelines that will direct you to a healthier and more effective course of action.

1. Don't Look for Instant Answers to Your Problems

Your first step in self-awareness is to slow down when you have a problem. Never rush to find the answer to a problem no matter how urgent it feels. For example, when you are in the middle of a crisis with your partner and you seek a solution to that crisis, you are likely to think and act impulsively because you are anxious and frightened. In such an emotionally charged state, any answer may seem better than nothing at all, but solutions arrived at in such emotional states only generate more problems down the road.

2. Stay with Your Feelings—Don't Run away from Them

Your second step is to absorb the experience and upset. You just feel it. You stay with it. You acknowledge it. You experience it and you don't ignore, minimize, deny, or judge the whirlwind of unsettling emotions that you feel. When you do not react to your immediate impulse to strike back, to defend yourself, or to somehow salvage your dignity with your partner, your total immersion in feeling all of your feelings allows the space to open up for a new vision and some clarity to settle into your consciousness.

You will find that your delay in reacting lets you take stock of the situation more clearly. It allows the time for your mind to "read" the messages that your emotions are sending. This is the true exercise of the sometimes difficult practice of impulse control, especially when you have been driven to an immediate hair-trigger response by your partner. Emotional impulse control is the key virtue that characterizes romantic intelligence.

3. Focus on Yourself, Not Your Partner

Your third step is to stay within yourself and your feelings. Don't wander away by focusing on your partner or the situation causing the emotional turmoil. To focus on your partner or the situation is to leave your feeling experience and its message, a message of self-awareness. For example, suppose your partner said something that hurt your feelings and you retaliated with a cutting remark of your own. You are angry and you try to think of the reasons why she was so hurtful to you. So, you come up with a story about her that justifies your behavior and your anger.

"She's so insensitive to my feelings." "No matter what I do for her it's never enough." "If she really loved me, she wouldn't talk that way to me." "She really doesn't love me and what she just said proves it." These thoughts are your "answer" to what happened, they are what your mind manufactures in the service of your righteous anger. In fact, these thoughts about her further intensify your emotions, causing you to distance yourself even more from the love you feel for her.

Instead of justifying your feelings with your thoughts, try staying only with your feelings by asking yourself, "What's inside me that's making me angry right now?" or "What's inside me that's making me hurt so bad right now?" You can substitute any emotion for this question and arrive at the honest answer that the emotion is trying to signal to you. Don't push or rush for an answer. Be patient. Allow the answer to your questions to surface without mental interference.

Usually, you will discover that your intense reaction is due to something greater than the current disagreement. For example, you may find that the fight you're having with your partner is but the latest in a series of incidents emerging from your past. Such incidents may have accumulated and been buried deep inside your psyche, only to be "sparked" by your current partner.

For instance, when somebody important in your past disapproved of or criticized you, you may have felt "bad" or unlovable then. Your partner's critical, harsh tone of voice and the critical message itself may have re-ignited your emotions from your past hurts. When you react before you think, you cause the conflict with your partner to escalate. When you react before you think, you are not *reading* your emotional signals, you are *reacting automatically* to them.

In this third step, take a deep breath to buy some time to calm your need to react immediately and, while breathing, direct your thoughts to your feelings so that an awareness of your reaction will come to your thoughts. Note that you may find your hard-won insight difficult to accept.

For instance, suppose you discover that when you are criticized you feel shame and embarrassment, because deep down within yourself you believe that any criticism must mean that there is something really wrong with you—so wrong that you are unlovable and can't ever be loved. If you can't be loved, then, eventually, your life partner will tire of you and dump you for someone else. When you make that connection, you then see that the issue is really your fear of abandonment, which you have associated with your partner's criticism.

With this insight you can make an emotional course correction and become able to connect with your partner in a reasonable, good-tempered way. If you choose to share the insight with your partner, you will lose your defensiveness. Such emotional honesty can only draw you closer together because your openness about such a painful subject will create a deeper intimacy with your partner.

4. Walk the Tightrope Between Thoughts and Feelings

Allowing yourself to be fully human and at one with yourself requires maintaining a strong balance between your ability to think clearly and your ability to feel deeply. When your mind and emotions are open and accessible to each other, working in unison, the interplay between thoughts and feelings creates a powerful clarity in your mind and actions. Such clarity is the best environment for clear, honest communication to take place between you and your partner.

Self-awareness is giving yourself permission and having the courage to look into the dark corners of your soul, uncensored, undistorted, and unadorned in your self-perceptions. Self-awareness is also having the courage to see your strengths and possibilities. To live up to your possibilities requires change; it requires seeing and doing things differently. It requires making tough decisions about moving on with your life.

When your self-esteem, your sense of competency, and the value you place on your accomplishments derive from the opinions of others, then anything that you feel or think becomes untrustworthy and to be ignored. You block your emotional signals, you lose your ability to live passionately and creatively, and you never experience the romantic intelligence that is your birthright.

5. Managing Your Emotions

To manage your emotions, the elements of empathy, impulse control, and anger management must be present. When you learn to slow down and think before you act, you are beginning to manage your emotions properly. Then you experience improvement in recognizing and naming your feelings. You become better able to understand the causes of your feelings, and you learn to recognize the difference between feelings and actions.

You also learn how to tolerate frustration better, and how to handle your anger. Anger management results in you becoming better able to express your anger appropriately, without fighting. You learn to use fewer verbal put-downs, and you don't get into fights. Less aggressive or self-destructive behavior is the result of more self-control in handling stress and being better able to pay attention and focus on the task at hand.

6. The Aftermath

Emotional self-awareness clears away any misconceptions you may have about who you are and how things should be; it strips away unrealistic wishful thinking and expectations that feed your needs for security and love. This new level of consciousness can be so unsettling and upsetting to your notions of how things are and should be that it is easy to run away from it back into the womb of false comfort. But if you want to develop your romantic intelligence, you must swallow your pride, take a deep breath, and stick with the experience that your insight brings to you.

Remember, self-awareness does not mean to live only in your emotions. To live *only* in your emotions, with little regard for the consequences of your actions, to be impulsive and do things without thinking and planning, just creates confusion and chaos in your life and in your relationships. It endangers you and alienates others. To live only in your emotions is acting and reacting without thought of the consequences. It is the loss of self-awareness.

Contact Your Inner Guide

The final step to becoming more self-aware is to make contact with the invisible presence or the intuitive voice inside you that guides and presides over your emotions. Your guide is not an external entity, an ancestor, or a ghostly presence from your past, but your own inner voice that whispers and counsels you, if you take the time and create the right space to listen. This voice can be comforting, instructive, driving, practical, impassioned, or enraged, depending on when, where, and how it comes to you. Many times, the voice is equated with a conscience that tells you what right and wrong are all about. Some call it "intuition." Some say it exists in the place between conscious emotions and unconscious emotions. Listen to your inner voice. Trust it and become familiar with the navigational signals that it sends to you to help you make your way in the world.

CHAPTER FIVE

CONQUER JEALOUSY AND ANGER WITH ROMANTIC INTELLIGENCE

*Self-control does not come from controlling
our feelings but from feeling our feelings.*

—Jeanne Segal, Ph.D.
Emotional Intelligence

No one is immune from experiencing and expressing toxic emotions. To feel anger, rage, jealousy, guilt, fear, depression, and grief is part of being human. They are manifestations of the darker side of life. When they are understood, expressed appropriately, and redirected, these emotions retain their toxic potential, but they also can be transformative; i.e., they can be powerful agents for change.

Even more than positive emotions, the toxic emotions can facilitate communication within a relationship and create a greater intimacy and deeper connection between partners. The intensity of these emotions, as uncomfortable as they are, forces you to face your problems. The extent of your romantic intelligence will determine whether you use these emotions to problem-solve or to damage your relationship.

When you are romantically intelligent, you don't ignore toxic emotions or run away from feeling them. You accept them, face them, and deal with them in appropriate ways. Toxic emotions and painful feelings are a part of any relationship. Reconfigure their potency and tap into their energy, and they will allow you to right a wrong, defend your personal boundaries, and feel better about yourself. Furthermore, after dealing with them, they have the potential to make your relationship grow stronger.

Do You Pick Up on Emotional Signals?

Many people don't express their feelings because they can't identify them while they are happening. This inability to pick up on your own emotions may occur because when you were socialized as a child, you learned which emotions are acceptable and which are not. You learned how to push unacceptable feelings such as anger and hurt out of your conscious awareness. So as an adult, you may fail to recognize them, even when you or your partner is feeling or expressing them. To further confuse the issue, some people smile when they're angry or frown when they're happy, and they don't even know they are sending contradictory signals.

How can you detect what you're feeling? It's easy. Just learn to read your own facial expressions and body language, and see what you look like when you feel an emotion. Rent a video with a lot of emotional content, and look at yourself in a mirror when you cry, laugh, or feel fear or anger. Your emotions and feelings are expressed in your body postures, the way you hold yourself, and in your facial expressions, even if you are not consciously aware of them.

If you are going through a hard time with your partner, you may find yourself rechanneling your emotions into neurotic behaviors like compulsive shopping, compulsive gambling, compulsive overeating, even compulsive sexual behavior, as a way of getting back at your partner for hurting you.

As a prelude to diving deeper into the toxic emotions, take a few minutes now and try to get in touch with either a strong positive emotion or a strong negative one. Any emotion will do, but especially strong ones will telegraph important messages. They are your personal "emotional beepers" or internal signals telling you that something is out of kilter either with yourself or with your situation. When you're emotionally "beeped" it means that you need to reflect on the emotion, but not try to act on it unthinkingly or impulsively. Remember, an important marker of the romantically intelligent person is impulse control.

EXERCISE: IDENTIFYING YOUR FEELINGS

1. Sit back in a comfortable position and close your eyes.

2. Think about a strong emotion or powerful feeling that you've experienced in the last couple of days. It can be either pleasant or unsettling.

3. What did you experience physically? What did you experience on the outer part of your body? What did you experience in the inner part of your body?

4. Ask yourself, "What did I do with this feeling?" "Did I ignore or deny it?" "Did I really understand the message that this feeling or emotion was telling me?" "Did I really deal with it the best I could?" "If not, why not?"

5. Now ask yourself. "What was the outcome of how I dealt with the feeling?" "Was the outcome helpful and satisfactory?" "If not, why not?"

Do this exercise frequently to become sensitive to your emotions and what they are telling you. With practice, you will become more strongly attuned to your own emotional signals; this will allow you to face problems far more quickly than in the past. You also will find that you cannot ignore, deny, or minimize your emotional experiences. Repeated practice will encourage you to problem-solve quickly, and will increase both your romantic intelligence and your sense of well-being.

Rewire Your Thinking about Emotional Toxicity

Your romantic intelligence will bloom when you begin to associate emotional toxicity and traditionally negative emotions with the need for change and mutual growth. You can reprogram your thoughts about toxic emotions even on a neurological level. When an emotion such as anger or jealousy comes up for you, immediately disconnect the feeling from its negative connotation, shift it to the positive connotation, and try to think about what it's trying to tell you. What does it really mean? Emotions like rage or depression tell you something is obviously wrong or troubling with your relationship or with you, and you need to deal with it. You and your partner can use these feelings as a starting point for addressing the problems. The following story is a good example of what can happen when your ignore the signals your emotions send to you.

Bobbie and David

Every evening when bedtime came around, Bobbie got angry, sullen, and depressed. She dreaded going to bed, and put off sleep by watching television or reading, while her partner, David, turned his back to her and fell asleep with the light still on. His distant, cold bedtime behavior had been going on for about three months, until one night, after dinner, he tenderly took her hand, and asked her to come to bed and hold him while he slept.

In the previous five years, they had slept in each other's arms every night. But three months earlier, David was assigned a stressful project with a tight deadline, and he had stopped cuddling her without telling her why he needed to sleep apart. She immediately assumed he no longer loved her. She didn't dare ask him why he had changed so abruptly, she was too afraid his answer would confirm her fears, she just got more and more depressed and angry.

David was on automatic pilot. To get his job done, he had to shut down all of his physical and emotional sensors. He couldn't think about anything except his job. He got up, went to work, came home, and went to sleep. Seven days a week. All this time, he never really saw Bobbie, never heard her voice, never even missed her touch. He was living entirely in his head and was so focused on work, it was as if she wasn't there. He certainly never thought to explain to her that he had withdrawn because he was so stressed out.

For her part, Bobbie never questioned her increasing anger or her depression, both of which were signaling loud and clear to her that David—and their relationship—needed some attention. Instead, she began to fantasize that he was having an affair with another woman, and would soon ask for a divorce. Since she didn't want to explore her feelings, and she didn't want to voice her fear that he had new lover, she just withdrew and got even angrier and more depressed.

After about three months of this, the pressure at David's job started winding down, and he began "waking up" to the other parts of his life. On his first weekend at home, he became aware of how emotionally disconnected he had become from himself and his partner. When he was in bed, he felt as if he were sleeping alone. As if awakening from a deep sleep, he started thinking about his relationship with Bobbie and he suddenly realized that his coldness and distancing behaviors must have wounded her deeply.

When David asked Bobbie to come to bed and hold him, she felt a sharp pain in her chest and began to cry. Her pain broke through the defenses she had built, and she found the courage to tell him what she had been feeling and thinking over the last three months. Then he started to cry.

Their truth-telling reunion went on for hours and when it was over they were both emotionally exhausted, but clear about their priorities. They promised to talk about their feelings regularly, no matter what else was happening in their lives, because they loved each other and valued their relationship. They both understood that they had just narrowly avoided doing terrible damage to their relationship. That night they slept in each other's arms again.

Their story is a classic case of emotional mismanagement. A lot of pain and grief could have been avoided if Bobbie had only paid close attention to the anger and depression she was feeling. She chose not to address her feelings and matters only got worse. Negative emotions are signals. They are messages that signal the need to communicate with your partner, not only to solve the issues that cause the negative feelings, but also to experience relief from those feelings. When communication is effective and the problem has been corrected, you draw closer to each other.

Avoid Guessing Games and Silence

The romantically intelligent person is comfortable, open, and expresses her feelings; she will tell her partner what she is feeling in order to create a deeper bond with him. Her partner will feel free to express what he feels, too. Feelings shared are not always pleasant. Sometimes the feelings are very negative. They can sting, as sharp as a wasp sting, but at least you will know what your partner is feeling and thinking.

This doesn't mean that you should use your emotions like a battering ram to get back at your partner; instead they should serve you like a compass to direct you to issues you and your partner need to discuss and resolve. To be emotionally withdrawn and not share your feelings will create distance and coldness between the two of you.

When there is distance and concealment, your partner has to try to guess what you are feeling. Guessing and false suppositions can lead to false conclusions and serious misunderstandings. To be romantically intelligent is to have all your channels of communication open, even though at times it will be painful. Painful disclosure is certainly easier to live with than the silent treatment, which can be the kiss of death for any relationship.

Watch Out for Emotions That Go On and On

Your romantic intelligence knows that negative emotions like anger, nervousness, and sadness can be helpful. However, they become damaging when their *duration* (how long they last) or their *intensity* (how strong they are) become excessive. For example, failing a test, losing out on a job you had your heart set on, not getting accepted at the school you hoped to attend, these are all events that naturally cause you to feel sad and depressed. However, when the sadness is over the loss or failure goes on and on without any end in sight, over months and months, that means you're stuck on an emotional treadmill that won't take you anywhere. Your emotions are just sapping your energy, causing you to limit your activities, and killing any spark to engage in something new. The same is true for chronic anger, habitual jealousy, or "rageholism," a condition where you become addicted to expressing intense anger because it makes you feel powerful and important.

Many couples don't share their feelings because it can create anxiety to be so direct in saying, "I'm angry," "I'm embarrassed," or even "I love you." Don't let this happen to you. Don't allow a buildup of hurts, slights, and misunderstanding to accumulate. Address them when they occur. Couples with high Romantic IQs know that the process of dealing with conflicts, and arriving at satisfactory resolutions, drives people together, not apart. To ignore and minimize relationship problems and put on a "happy face" when you are not happy, is to build an unconscious but dense wall of resentment and distance between yourself and your partner. The wall may become impenetrable and the relationship will collapse.

Beware of Mind Reading

To be romantically intelligent is to understand that neither you nor your partner is a mind reader. For example, if you are frustrated or angry with your partner because she seems to be ignoring you, or you feel that she's not supportive enough, it's possible that you're contributing to the problem by failing to tell her how *you* feel. You may have the expectation that she should know how you feel and be sensitive to your needs without you having to tell her.

But it's unrealistic to expect your partner to read your feelings and your thoughts. As close as your partner is to you, he can't always pick up on what's going on with you, just as you can't aleways pick up on what's going on with him. All of us can be insensitive at times, so you must be willing to tell your partner what you're feeling. Awareness comes from communicating feelings and thoughts, not the expectation that your partner will magically know what you need and what you're feeling.

Think about a parent's frustration trying to figure out the cause of an infant's distress. Does her crying mean she wants to be fed, changed, or burped? If you don't tell your partner what's wrong, you put your partner in the same place as parents who have to read their baby's mind. But unlike a baby, you can speak. You need to spell things out, you need to tell your partner what you need, from how you like your eggs cooked to how you like to be touched.

To be romantically intelligent is also to understand that full disclosure about your needs, feelings, and desires requires unceasing practice. Practicing open communication and making your needs known throughout your relationship is to learn to know each other better and, in the process, you will grow closer to each other.

Managing Your Emotions

Although the romantically intelligent person reads her inner emotional signals very clearly, she is able to intercede between what she feels and how she *discharges* her emotions by her behavior. She knows that feeling a strong emotion doesn't mean it should be expressed in destructive and hurtful ways. She understands it does mean that something's happened to upset her that must be addressed. The ability to control behavior when emotions are intense is characteristic of the person with romantic intelligence—she exhibits excellent impulse control.

To be romantically intelligent you must know what to do with your emotions to make your relationship better, not worse. There are the positive feelings of love, joy, pleasure, desire, warmth, and tenderness. These emotions strengthen your relationship and make life worth living. There are also problematic emotions that create the mutual awareness of needs, wishes, and issues. These are a matter of how you think about your feelings. Your thoughts contribute to regulating how and what you feel, and for how long. You may not always recognize your self-talk, that is, how you talk to yourself about what you are feeling, but it's always there, influencing your emotions and moods.

EXERCISE: THE EFFECTS OF THOUGHTS ON YOUR EMOTIONS

This exercise will reveal what your inner thoughts are telling you and how you should respond emotionally.

1. Sit back in a comfortable chair and close your eyes. Make sure there are no distractions or disruptions as you relax.

2. For the next five minutes, listen to the voice that you use when you think—your "thinking voice" or self-talk. You may be saying, "What voice?" Keep trying, and continue making an effort to hear your inner thoughts.

3. Now, create the following scenarios in your mind. Pay attention to your thoughts and the emotions that follow them.

Scenario 1: Imagine you're having a very engaging conversation on the phone with your partner, who's a very patient and good listener. Suddenly, he cuts the conversation short by saying, "Sorry but I have to get off the phone now." And with that, he hangs up. What's your reaction to this abrupt ending? What do you say to yourself? Do you find that what you say to yourself affects your feelings? What feelings do you experience?

Scenario 2: You come home after a long day at work. Your partner greets you with a smile and asks you how your day has been. After telling her, you ask her how her day has been, and she says "fine," and abruptly walks away into another room. What is your reaction? What do say to yourself? What kinds of feelings do your thoughts create for you?

Scenario 3: It's Saturday night and you're ready to go out to dinner and a movie with your partner. Your plans were made beforehand. Suddenly, just before going out, your partner has a change of heart and tells you that he doesn't want to go out; he would rather stay home. He says to you that, if you like, you can go out alone. What's your reaction to his sudden turnaround? What do you think to yourself? What do you feel?

Describe the various emotions and feelings that you are experiencing right now. Are they mixed? Intense? Mild? What do you feel like saying, based on what you're thinking and feeling?

These three scenarios are somewhat ambiguous situations open to interpretation. What you feel and the emotional intensity of your feeling depend on your reading of the situation. For example, if you completely personalize the experiences above, you will feel slighted, angry, and hurt—critical of your partner's behavior. You would feel that your partner has failed you because he's not meeting your expectations of how he should behave with you.

If you're feeling depressed and guilty, then it's likely that you feel that there's something wrong with you that causes her to act that way. In this instance, you take the full blame for her behavior; in the former situation, you would have blamed your partner. Remember, your thoughts determine which emotions you will feel, and your emotions will govern your reactions and behavior.

You Are Responsible for Your Emotions

As a romantically intelligent person *you and you alone are responsible for your feelings and emotions*. Make sure that this sense of responsibility is reflected in what you say to your partner. Instead of saying, "You make me angry," say instead, "I'm getting angry." Instead of saying to your partner, "You hurt me," say instead, "I felt hurt when you did that." In this way, you tell yourself and your partner that you *own* your emotions and feelings.

Such acknowledgement does not trigger the negative response that you would surely get from your partner if he felt that you blamed him for what you feel. Increasing your responsibility for how you think, act, and feel indicates that your romantic intelligence is improving and working well.

Emotions and Health

The romantically intelligent person values physical well-being. To express emotions appropriately means that you release the physical tensions that reside in your body when you feel strong emotions. If you ignore, block, or deny your emotions, you will put yourself into a state of constant stress and tension. Unexpressed emotions can furrow your brow, pinch your nerves, place a hammerlock around your neck, literally twist your intestines, cause chest pains, and on and on. Massage therapists and other bodyworkers run lucrative businesses because so many people allow their bodies to absorb their emotions, rather than letting them flow in and out. This is why partners in a healthy relationships enjoy better health than those in dysfunctional relationships.

Are You the Jealous Type?

Imagine you and your lover are walking in the mall. You see a great outfit in the window of your favorite shop and you ask him if he minds waiting, while you go in and try it on. He says he'll "people watch" on the bench, and meet you when you come out. You buy the outfit, go back, and see your lover standing there with his arms around a stranger. They are hugging and kissing in such a way that you know they have been intimately connected. You see their mutual excitement and pleasure at seeing each other, and you just stand there flushed and shaking, until he sees you and breaks away from her.

At that moment, you have several choices. You can let your imagination run wild and become convinced that your lover is having a secret affair, you can panic and flee, you can erupt in an angry outburst, or you can try to calm down. Naturally, the reality of the scene is upsetting. Seeing their lover in what can only be construed as a romantic embrace with another person will ignite jealousy in most people.

Before you take an emotional leap or jump to false conclusions, you can take three deep breaths, walk up to the couple, and calmly make your presence known. Let your partner explain the situation. Take some more time to process what he says and your emotions. Take some more deep breaths. In most cases, your worst fears will be baseless; she will turn out to be someone he knew ages ago: his girlfriend in high school, his best friend's kid sister, someone he cares about, but, clearly, no threat to your relationship.

Jealousy is one of the most toxic emotions you can experience, because it is a combination of feelings. It is anger plus other emotions. Among the several emotions that may go into creating jealousy are fear, anxiety, hurt, helplessness, insecurity, possessiveness, rivalry, vengefulness, self-blame, and the threat of abandonment. Since relationships are built on strong emotions and not "arrangements" between two people, when your partner relates to others in an intimate manner, then threats to your relationship are perceived easily, and may be very frightening.

Your status as Number One in your partner's eyes seems threatened, especially if you are not emotionally mature and you feel insecure within yourself and your relationship. There is a strong possessive quality to jealousy. But possessiveness strikes at the heart of personal development, independence, and the freedom your partner needs to become the person he wants to be. If you are not growing yourself, your partner's growth might seem threatening you, so you might become jealous, limiting his relationships and experiences with others, monitoring his activities, and accusing him of being unfaithful and betraying your trust.

If your partner *is* attracted to someone else, jealousy can erupt with sudden and extreme severity. But if your partner is loyal to your relationship nothing will come of it. People do become attracted to others; it's part of life's erotic play. But that doesn't mean your partner will act on this attraction. However, if you are prone to jealousy, you might jump to exaggerated conclusions about what you think your partner is doing now and might do in the future. Your feelings about your partner are the issue, not your partner.

When you are jealous, everything is a forgone conclusion for you: You are sure your importance in your partner's eyes has been diminished. You are certain that you will lose him if you don't put a stop to his "extracurricular" activities. Because of your fears and insecurities, losing him is the only future you can envision. It may have nothing to do with reality, but it has everything to do with being jealous.

To be jealous means you try to manipulate your partner's relationships with others. If you tell your partner how jealous you feel about her friendship with someone else, she may feel so bad about it that she will end the relationship to make you feel more secure and less jealous. The problem is that jealousy can become a never-ending response to every friendship your partner has, and eventually she will feel suffocated by your demands and the very thing you fear will happen; she will leave you. In other words, jealousy creates its own self-fulfilling prophecies.

Jealousy Can Be All-Embracing

Jealousy of your partner can go beyond his relations with others. It can extend into all kinds of other areas, such as getting job promotions, earning honors while attending school, engaging in travel, recreational, or cultural activities.... This list could be as endless as jealousy itself.

Jealousy is always about a lack of or loss of ego: you imagine that someone else is more appealing than you or someone else possesses what you don't have. You think, "Why am I not as attractive to him as she is?" "What does he have that I don't have?" Jealousy is about the threat of future loss. It also says, "Look at me. Hello, I'm here." Normal jealousy, according to Freud, is compounded with grief—the thought of losing the one you love, and the imagining of the narcissistic wound that the loss will cause your ego. Jealousy also involves self-criticism and the implication that you're not as good as, not as rich as, not as appealing as. . . . You can be jealous of another adult, children, a job, even a pet.

Jealousy Can Become Paranoia

When you feel jealousy, you are totally focused on your partner's activities and whereabouts. You become hypervigilant, looking for the slightest clue that your partner is straying and is no longer interested in you. The toughest part of dealing with jealousy is having to face yourself. If your relationship is troubled, examining the origins of your jealousy is important. Usually, jealousy has its origins in abandonment issues from your past that have become re-ignited in the present. When your partner spends time with others, you may feel rejected and displaced.

The difficult truth to face is this: Yes, there are times when your partner does prefer someone else to you. This does not mean that he will leave you. It does mean that as close and as committed as you are to each other, you cannot possibly fulfill all of his needs for stimulation and variety. This is a fact of life you must realize, come to terms with, and accept.

Some people hide their jealousy by pretending that nothing is wrong, so their partners won't have a clue as to how jealous they really are. In situations like these, the jealous partners may become self-destructive and really threaten the relationship by having extramarital affairs (the "I'll show him!" syndrome) and provoking fights with their partners over any issue as a cover up for their jealousy.

To be romantically intelligent is to know that jealousy is not just in your head but also in your feelings. The more secure you are, the more self-esteem you have, the less jealousy you will feel. There are some people who experience no jealousy at all. For most of us, though, it's a matter of degree. The amount of jealousy and its intensity vary a great deal among couples.

Jealousy and Love

Jealousy has nothing to do with love. Rather, jealousy is an emotional yardstick that relates to your self-esteem. Beware of your partner saying, "Yes, I'm jealous because I love you so much." This declaration of love is intended to flatter you into thinking that your partner's need to control and restrict your activities is due to his (or her) great love for you. To equate love with jealousy implies that love means giving up all the other important parts of your life for your lover. But love doesn't mean that you should give up your dreams or suffocate your spirit. A partner's jealousy can destroy the pleasure of being alive; it can be so overwhelming that you lose your ability to simply be yourself.

To be romantically intelligent is to know that you have a committed relationship with your partner, that you both love and care about each other, that you prefer to be with each other most of the time—but not all of the time. When you are romantically intelligent you know this truth in your gut, and you are not threatened by it. In fact, you know your partner's freedom to be herself, to do things independently, to strike out on her own, only strengthens your bond.

When you respect your partner's independence and support his activities, he will love you all the more because he will be even more fulfilled. Life for both of you will become far more meaningful when you support your partner's enthusiasms and choices in life, instead of trying to restrict them.

Kim's Romantically Intelligent Choice

Kim had a choice: stay with her live-in lover and endure his constant vigilance or move out and eventually find another lover who would allow her to spend time with other people and encourage her to grow and develop herself. She worked two jobs: the first as a personal trainer at a gym, and the other at a hair salon, where she was studying to become a hair stylist. She dreamt about combining these two skills one day and opening her own health salon.

Kim was outgoing, cheerful, personable, and loved going places and having fun, but for three years, her boyfriend Jerry had been putting the brakes on her dreams and succeeding in keeping her at home nights, far away from her friends. He called her five times a day at work, monitored her e-mail, and refused to acknowledge his controlling behavior or jealousy. She had tried to discuss these issues with him, but his response was always along the lines that a "normal woman" would not want any other company than the man she lived with.

Kim admitted she was with Jerry "for security." "It was nice to have someone to come home to at night, to share expenses, and to go to parties with, although he didn't like me to talk to anyone else." She had been married once when she was very young and, at twenty-nine, she wanted to expand her world and meet other men, but she was afraid to give up her "security" and strike out on her own, even if meant putting up with Jerry's rules and controlling behavior.

Finally, after months of continual quarreling, she got over her fear, and rented her own apartment. When she told Jerry what she had done, he refused to visit her after she moved out. He finally relented, though, and they are becoming friends again. Kim is living alone. Money is tight and she does not feel as financially secure as she did when she lived with Jerry, but she is happy and working on her career. For the first time in her life she is dating a variety of men and hasn't made a precipitous commitment to any of them.

How to Handle Jealousy in Your Relationship

If the jealousy in your relationship is not severe but is still a problem, it can be modified. Here are some solutions:

☆ If you are the partner who evokes jealousy, you must assure your partner that you love her and value her company and ideas. Show more affection. Leave her notes telling her that you love her. Surprise her with gifts. The important idea is for your partner to know that she is loved and special.

☆ If you are the jealous person, you crave assurances that you are loved and special. You also know that your jealousy intensifies if you feel you are being ignored or discounted. You need constant reassurance that you are loved, and when love is offered to you, you should allow yourself to feel loved.

☆ The best way to handle jealousy is to confront it honestly and see it as something that needs to be managed and changed. You and your partner can and should discuss the specific wounds you both received from rejection, abandonment, and other painful events that may be part of your personal histories. Working on jealousy honestly and lovingly is a difficult process, but it can bring two people closer together than they were before.

The most intense form of jealousy develops when your partner is extremely dependent on you, emotionally and socially. If your partner develops and values his independence, and he is not totally reliant on you for his emotional and social nourishment, the less jealous he will be. Being romantically intelligent is to take pride in your partner's independence, his ability to have his own circle of friends, interests, and projects. Increasing self-reliance decreases jealousy considerably and causes it to lose its sharp bite.

Severe Jealousy

If your partner's jealousy is severe and unrelenting, that is, when you must give your partner an accounting for everything you do every day, and no matter what you do to solve the problem, it always fails, then this situation has to be taken to the bottom line. To regain your life, you must lose the relationship. You must tell your jealous partner that you will no longer live your life in fear, that you will live your life on your own terms not his. You can say, "Yes, I am leaving you for someone else. I am leaving you for myself."

Although this approach may seem extremely harsh, remember this: When you cave in to your jealous partner's false beliefs about you, you only succeed in reinforcing those false beliefs. Although leaving the relationship may appear harsh and extreme, remember this: when you are continually forced to try to prove that you are innocent of your jealous partner's false beliefs about you (that you are not loyal, or are cheating), you succeed only in reinforcing those false beliefs. No matter what you say or do, your partner will always be suspicious of you and never trust you or take you at your word. There simply is no end to this loop; anything you say or do to prove your loyalty to your partner will be futile.

EXERCISE: If Jealousy Is a Problem for You

If you experience frequent bouts of jealousy with your partner and you find that it's hurting your relationship with him, ask yourself this question. What exactly does your partner do to make you feel jealous?: Here are some of the questions you can ask yourself to get started:

- ♥ Is it that he doesn't spend enough time with you?

- ♥ Is it when he spends time with his friends?

- ♥ Do you feel jealous when your partner is at work?

- ♥ Do you experience jealousy when you are at parties and social gatherings with your partner?

♥ Do you feel twinges of jealousy when your partner talks on the phone with someone you don't know?

♥ What do you experience when someone tries to flirt with your partner?

♥ What do you feel when your partner spends time with his parents or siblings, and you are not with them?

After you have answered the questions above, then ask yourself these questions:

♥ Is there hard evidence that your partner may be becoming discontented and resentful when with you, and prefers the company of others to yours?

♥ If your partner says no to your suspicions do you believe him? Remember, just being with others is not enough to tell you that he is discontented with you, even though you may feel otherwise if you're feeling jealous.

♥ Do you question your partner's loyalty and commitment to you?

♥ When he does say he is loyal to you and committed to your relationship, do you believe him? If you do not, what is your hard proof that he is not being truthful?

♥ Do you believe your partner when he says he loves and cares about you?

♥ Are you suspicious of his motives for doing things?

After you answer the question above, think about your answers to the next question:

♥ Are you drawing conclusions about your partner's behavior by filling in the missing pieces and jumping to your own conclusions based on what you feel?

♥ If you can't trust your partner to tell you the truth, even when he tells you the truth, *then you have a relationship problem that must be addressed.*

When you are feeling jealous, no amount of reasoning will suffice. No matter what your partner tells you, you'll never believe him. The same holds true if you're a victim of his jealousy. You will find it next to impossible to convince your partner that you are loyal and are not having dalliances with someone else.

If Jealousy Is a Problem for Your Partner

If your partner is jealous, it's not just his or her problem—it's your problem too. A jealous partner can hold you hostage, curtail your activities, and stifle your life. Before you discuss the problem with your partner or take even more radical steps, take an inventory of how your partner's jealousy is affecting your life. Answer the following questions to determine how intrusive or disruptive the problem is.

★ How many times a day does your partner check up on you via e-mail, telephone, cell phone, or through your secretary?

★ How is the jealousy expressed? Does she tell you? Does she become angry if you speak to someone else? Does she make snide comments if you are on the phone with someone?

★ Do you feel free to converse with colleagues, friends, and business associates of the opposite sex or do you hold back for fear of offending your partner?

★ Does your partner insist on knowing your whereabouts at all times? Does she check up on you or try to trap you into telling a lie?

★ Does your partner test your loyalty to her?

★ Has jealousy always been a problem, or is this a recent phenomenon in your relationship?

The more detailed and comprehensive your answers are, the quicker you will be able to figure out how deep the problem is. In your journal, record how your partner's jealousy makes you feel. Does it enrage you? Does it make you want to distance yourself or even leave the relationship? Knowing exactly how jealousy feels—being able to express how it feels in words and sentences—will help you to communicate with your partner about these issues.

Anger: The Emotional Umbrella

Anger is an emotion that that we all experience at different times and in various strengths. It is an uncomfortable, controversial, powerful, and helpful or destructive emotion, depending to how you relate to it and how you work with it. In many instances, anger is an "umbrella" emotion that covers and disguises other emotions as well. For example, frequently anger incorporates hurt, confusion, resentment, jealousy, frustration, disappointment, betrayal, shame, and embarrassment. Anger is so strong an emotion that it breaks through any walls of timidity that you might display. When you are truly angry and you lack the courage to speak your mind, your body language will express your anger and "speak up" for you.

Accepting Anger

The *acceptance* of anger is to recognize it when it occurs and, as best as you can, let it be. If you stop judging, denying, or belittling your emotions, including anger, you become more accepting of yourself in the process. Self-acceptance leads to greater self-esteem and self-confidence because you learn to accept all the parts of yourself. You accept those qualities that make you human, make you frail, and make you strong; you acknowledge those parts of yourself that limit your options and possibilities, and those that expand your possibilities. When you become more self-accepting you naturally become less defensive and less self-protective.

Instead of building your self-concept on a foundation based on your insecurities and fears, you construct a self based on your experiences, a self-concept more closely aligned to the actual person you are. Knowing yourself well is a very powerful aid, because you can draw from your actual experiences those strengths and qualities that create greater depth, fulfillment, and happiness in relationship.

To be romantically intelligent is to be strongly self-accepting. The more accepting of yourself you are, the more accepting you are of others. Accepting the fact of anger is so important because it is difficult to make peace with it; it threatens your view of your capacity for kindness and love for others. When you don't accept your anger, you begin to doubt your patience and tolerance for all the things that irritate you, or you create pain. Not feeling threatened by the intensity of your own anger is a sure sign of greater maturity. The paradox of anger is the more you accept it, the more you recognize who you are.

Anger Requires Impulse Control

Anger requires control, for you cannot express your anger at will, whenever you choose. You must consider your partner's feelings, moods, and activities at the moment. To vent your anger at will impulsively, because you feel uncomfortable with what you're feeling, is to overwhelm your partner to the point where any meaningful communication becomes impossible. To be romantically intelligent, you accept and connect with your anger when you experience it. Any form of emotional pain that derives from your past (whether distant or recent) is anger.

Anger serves a twofold purpose: to protect you from further pain and to allow the emotional pain that you do have to be discharged from your body. If you hold on to anger, it becomes more intense, and you will explode at the slightest provocation. If you store up your anger for long periods of time, it becomes disconnected from its original source of pain, your anger becomes generalized, and you are angry most of the time. At this point, your anger builds even more momentum and you find yourself becoming even angrier because you're angry.

EXERCISE: LEARN TO CONTROL YOUR ANGER

♥ The next time you become angry with your partner, think before you act. If you feel that you've been provoked into anger, take several deep breaths immediately and consciously hold on to your emotional reins.

♥ By controlling your first angry impulses, you buy time between the moment your anger ignites and the need to lash out. While you are taking deep breaths, the intensity of your anger lessens and you can gain more control of your behavior.

♥ If possible, take a time-out. Leave the room. Do something to lower your stress level. Listen to some music or do some exercise. Let some time go by.

♥ Only when your partner is ready and receptive to talk, and not a moment before, start to discuss and problem-solve the situation that has made you angry. Do this the next time your partner provokes you.

♥ Remember, if you vent your anger indiscriminately, without regard to your partner's sensitivities, you will only make the situation worse.

To be romantically intelligent is to create a balance between expressing your feelings and restraining them. You restrain your anger so you can read the message your anger is sending you. In the process of reading the message, your anger will lose some of its edge. This dissipation allows you to see what the anger contains and covers up. Underneath your anger, do you feel let down, hurt, or disappointed by your partner? Are you frustrated? If so, when the time is right, and when you both agree to discuss matters, you will find that when you deal with yourself first about the reasons for your anger, your words will have more power. Your communication with your partner will be richer and deeper, rather than argumentative, hostile, and combative.

If, on the other hand, you turn your emotional valve to "off," the anger builds up inside you; it becomes more intense and affects how you think and view your partner. Every thought, every feeling becomes exaggerated, distorted, and extreme. You begin to "see" that your partner has the worst characteristics imaginable, and you wonder what you saw in her in the first place. As you continue to close down your emotional spigot, keeping your anger to yourself, meaningful communication disappears and you create distance and coldness in your relationship. If such emotional withdrawal becomes the usual way you deal with your anger, this will cause the eventual death of your relationship.

Remember, by using your romantic intelligence, working with powerful emotions, and exerting your impulse control, you can transform anger, jealousy, and pain into empowerment and energy.

CHAPTER SIX

EMOTIONAL COMPATIBILITY

*The kind of man I like is an individual who has
not done the tidy and expected thing at every turn.
Those men have baggage up the wazoo.*

—Jean in Portland

If you plug the words "compatibility in relationships" into a search engine like Lycos or Google, it will come up with at least fifteen pages of Web sites to satisfy your quest for the perfect mate. Most of these sites are astrologically oriented (find out if the stars say that you are meant for each other); or they compare biorhythms, offer compatibility quizzes, decipher enneagrams, read tarot cards, or give psychic readings. These consultations are always guaranteed to determine whether you are a well-matched couple, or star-crossed lovers fated by the universe to remain apart.

Romantic compatibility is a recent invention; it is a twentieth-century phenomenon. Having your emotional needs met through marriage or a committed relationship was unheard of until modern times. In the past, issues of compatibility did not test relationships. They were built on culturally prescribed roles, not romance. Sometimes married couples would discover that they were emotionally compatible and fall in love within their relationship; other couples were not so lucky. But it didn't matter much. Emotional compatibility was not an issue. The purposes of relationships were to procreate, survive, and prosper, thus producing the material wealth needed for survival. Romantic love and romance were relegated to dalliances outside of marriage. Furthermore, being compatible referred to a couple's ethnic and religious backgrounds, and to the traditional gender differences that required clear-cut roles for men and women, not to emotional compatibility.

Today, compatibility is more *relational,* more dependent on highly personal characteristics such as the couple's likes and dislikes, habits, shared experiences and values, and similar outlooks on life. Large, extended families no longer support and reinforce relationships, nor do they provide emotional, financial, and child-rearing support. Today—to an unprecedented degree—most couples carry the emotional burdens of their relationships on their own shoulders. Without the support of extended families and close-knit communities, the pressure on a couple's relationship can be extraordinary.

What Causes Mutual Attraction?

You are naturally more attracted by, and more attractive to, someone who is more like you than not. Assets that top the list of desirable qualities are good physical, mental, and emotional health, being fairly well adjusted, and resilience. Others factors include having similar educational backgrounds, parents who are good role models, and mutual agreement between each other's expectations of what being in an intimate and engaged relationship means.

Certain qualities enhance a person's chances for success and compatibility in a relationship. A warm, emotionally expressive person is naturally attractive, and someone who has your same take on life, similar opinions, beliefs, attitudes, values, and so forth, will also be appealing. Outgoing, fun-loving people are attracted to other fun-loving people, and more introverted people seek their same kind of person. However, within a certain acceptable range of differences, pairs of opposites work, too; but if your partner holds strong religious, political, or lifestyle opinions contrary to yours, the going can get rough.

You are also more attracted to people who can meet your needs, as well as those you would like to care for and support. Most people prefer a partner who is capable, competent, and self-assured rather than a person who is needy, dependent, and lacking in self-confidence and self-esteem.

For most of us, difficult people are a turnoff. Consequently, easygoing and agreeable partners are more attractive than "high-maintenance" types. However, in the long run, the perfect partner for you may not be the most attractive, but the person who seems most human; someone with strong positive qualities who also makes mistakes and is not ashamed to admit them.

Honesty is a strong component of attraction in a relationship. When you are honest, you speak your mind, positively and negatively. Because of the feelings that are expressed in honest communication and their feedback, the relationship becomes more vital and, consequently, more meaningful. Emotional honesty is the essential element in the romantically intelligent couple's relationship. Lack of honesty, which results from trying to avoid conflict, creates resentments and builds distance with your partner.

The "HIM Manifesto"

Jean, in her thirties, is the divorced mother of two children. In the several years since her divorce, she has met a lot of men, but she hasn't found a partner with whom she could spend her life. So she decided to take the romantically intelligent approach to her next serious relationship. Her first step was to create the "HIM Manifesto," a list of qualities and conditions she finds desirable in a partner.

At first, Jean balked at the exercise. She said, "In some ways I'm squandering my time writing about these thoughts." Then, as she became more honest and self-aware, she wrote: "I think the truth is that I want to run away, and not think about who the person I am looking for is. I want to deny that I am interested in looking (am I?), and I have a screwed up notion that the way life works is that I will get zonked over the head by love, and I will fall into a perfect relationship with a great guy—ba-ba-boom, la la la." Of course, this belief ran counter to the evidence, and to her experience. So, she continued on and wrote, "Therefore, as I am a sensible person, I shall now define the type of man (my heart rate is jacking up and I am getting nervous) with whom I would be interested in having a relationship."

This is Jean's list:

★ Employed and successful in an established and valid business

★ Over 30 and under 65

★ Loyal

★ Honest

★ Kind and openhearted

★ Athletic in a casual sporty way—not currently a professional athlete

★ Healthy sense of humor about self, life, others

★ Loves children

★ Enjoys my kooky friends

★ Loves sex with an open and energetic attitude

★ Likes cats and dogs

★ Loves living life

Observe the specificity in Jean's list. Obviously, she has given a lot of thought to her relationships, and she has come up with a list of preferences that reflect her wishes, needs, and previous mistakes. You may find it unromantic to calculate what you want, but engaging in an exercise like this will reveal your needs to yourself, as well as the kind of partner you desire.

EXERCISE: THE TOP TEN DESIRABLE QUALITIES IN A PARTNER

On your computer, or in your journal or notebook, create a top ten list of the qualities you look for (or have) in a partner. After you have come up with at least ten, begin to prioritize the list. Number the qualities according to which has the greatest attraction for you. If you have a partner, this list will tell you what drew you both together, and it will illustrate your commonalties. If you are looking for a partner, the list will reveal your priorities and values.

Romantically Intelligent Compatibility

Romantically intelligent compatibility means mastering the art of relating to your partner through shared experiences, beliefs, and values, that is, how you act and think, particularly how you relate to each other through your emotions. Even though you may have divergent views in certain areas and you may do things differently, in general, you are well matched because you share empathy, respect, and an emotionally healthy approach to problem-solving.

The happiest relationships occur when two people with similar strengths come together and forge a bond based on mutual respect. Their love is also their quest to grow and evolve as individuals and as a couple. Personal development and the continuing evolution of their relationship are of paramount importance. There are also couples who are compatible because each partner shores up the other's weaknesses. This good deficit match makes both partners feel strong and accomplished. For example, when a controlling person pairs up with a dependent person, the couple may form a solid connection based on the compatibility of two opposites fulfilling each other's needs.

Do You Think Alike?

Laura, a New York City physician, had only one requirement when she put an ad into the personals column of her city's alternative paper. Her prospective date must be a regular reader of *The Village Voice,* but the *Boston Phoenix* was also acceptable. Laura's strategy, which targeted another reader with similar tastes in political reporting, worked. Mark answered her ad, and he and Laura conducted an extensive e-mail relationship in which they discovered that their separate lives had had some uncanny commonalties. They began spending time together, and found that their relationships with their parents, their value systems, and their basic attitudes about life matched up well. Six years of marriage and three children later, they are still compatible and very much in love.

Compatibility might or might not have been a matter of luck in this case, but Laura was on the right track when she placed her ad. In it, Laura was trying to find someone whose philosophy, political views, and approach to life meshed with hers. Her search targeted guys who read certain newspapers, which most likely meant bookish, educated men with liberal politics. That it worked out so well is miraculous, given the probability of making a compatible match.

Educational Issues

Compatibility usually relates to education, social class, and intelligence, although a carpenter and a debutante can live happily ever after if they click emotionally and intellectually. Intellectual compatibility increases your capacity for mutual understanding of life and each other. When you are intellectually compatible, you may understand each other's worldview, but not necessarily agree with it. Such broad understanding enhances any relationship's chance for survival. It's not a matter of formal education but of how you both think and interact emotionally that counts.

When partners have received equivalently high formal educations, their chances of achieving romantic intelligence increase. The greater earning power that higher education confers, and the choices that accompany having enough money, allow for an emotional stability in which two people can grow and support each other. This is a very different emotional climate than a couple with less earning power has. A less well-off couple must survive with the limited prospects, financial frustrations, and the difficult lifestyle that having fewer economic options entails. Highly educated, well-to-do partners have more options in the marketplace, more resources, and greater freedom to pursue their ambitions.

When the educational levels of a couple vary, one partner may be threatened by the other's higher education and greater number of options and choices. This is not to say a couple with large differences in their formal education cannot achieve romantic intelligence. It is to say, however, that if there are such large differences, it can be more difficult to achieve, because educational compatibility is just one more issue the partners must deal with.

Communication Issues

Compatibility in communication is not just a matter of using the same voice tone and communication style. It also refers to how much or how little a person says and to a mutually agreed-upon understanding of terms. For example, have you ever spent any time with someone who can't tolerate silence? He or she talks incessantly and never listens. They chatter to fill up empty conversational spaces. Or, have you ever been with someone who constantly withdraws and refuses to talk about anything at all with you? Clearly, in a close relationship, each partner's language skills have an effect on how the partners feel about their compatibility with each other.

Semantic Compatibility

Semantic compatibility refers to the way each partner understands certain relational concepts. For instance, for one person, "fidelity" may mean that he or she should never think about or interact with a person of the opposite sex. For another person, "fidelity" may mean that every kind of sexual activity is permitted with others except sexual intercourse. Still other people separate fidelity into different areas, such as physical or emotional fidelity.

Kenny and Dina: Culturally Out of Sync?

Kenny dated Dina for five years. They lived apart because if Dina had moved in with him, she would have been called a *putana* (prostitute) by the members of her large Italian family. Dina's life revolved around her huge family. There was a grandmother who had to be paid homage to on weekly Sunday visits, and more than a dozen aunts, uncles, and all their children. Kenny says that during their courtship the requirements to spend time with her family were much less demanding, but after they married, Dina's familial obligations used up every minute they weren't working. Kenny, whose own family is close but "not so enmeshed or demanding," became convinced that his needs always came in second after Dina's family's needs.

Today, looking back after their divorce, Kenny sees that he and Dina were never compatible. Early on, he insisted that they see a marriage counselor. Dina agreed, reluctantly, but after she discovered the therapist would not support her views about her duties to her family, she walked out.

Kenny said, "We had what I would describe as a task-oriented partnership. We connected with household tasks, but little else. At the time, I was studying Indian music, and she would make fun of my playing. She said that what I played sounded weird, 'like a bee stuck in a bottle.'" He also said that Dina was possessive and jealous. He had a job at a women's college playing piano for the dance classes, and Dina became obsessed about the dancers, insisting that he was involved with a student. "I was never interested in any of the dancers. My relationships with them were technical. I had to focus on the rhythms and make sure the music supported their movements, and made them look good."

Before Dina made good on her threat to throw his instruments out of their second-story window, Kenny decided to move out. "I realize now that moving out from under my bad marriage was a very important turning point in my life. I was finally asserting myself. I have a very high tolerance for bad emotional situations."

Dina's traditional value system and Kenny's nontraditional values set the stage for an emotionally incompatible match. They were out of sync culturally, psychologically, and emotionally. The chasm between them was too wide to negotiate. Kenny used his romantic intelligence when he made the decision to protect himself. He doesn't blame Dina for her different set of values; he just knew that they would both lead happier, more productive lives with other partners.

Having romantic intelligence means that you accept your partner's differences. It doesn't mean you necessarily like them, but you accept them—or you move on. The choice is yours. You can accept your partner's differences and make peace with many irritating behaviors, because the rewards of the overall relationship outweigh the irritations, or you can decide that your partner's differences are unacceptable, and move on.

Pack Rats and Neat Freaks

When you're working with romantic intelligence, you have a strong sense of the changes your partner reasonably can be expected to make, as well as the adjustments you can make for your partner's greater comfort. You also know that there are areas of disagreement that will always remain unresolved. The issue may be framed this way: Can you live with those disagreements and still keep the relationship vital and flourishing, or do you feel that you cannot agree to disagree?

In any case, it is fairly certain that there will be issues where you'll both need to give in a little to reach the middle ground, and to dilute any unpleasantness that may linger after you have had a difference of opinion. Remember, to be romantically intelligent is to be aware that the differences you and your partner have today relate to the differences you experienced growing up in your respective families. Because you understand that differences are not moral judgments, you don't view them as right or wrong behavior, only as differences in perspective, related to upbringing.

Sally and Joe: The Odd Couple

Sally and Joe were a well-matched couple. Both were bright, ambitious, well educated, and professionally successful. They shared many of the same interests and enjoyed each other's company. When they started living together, however, to their dismay, they discovered they were the "Odd Couple." Sally had grown up in a household that looked like a page out of *Better Homes and Gardens*. Joe said that he was "never a neat freak." He had always seen himself as having a "casual" lifestyle. Joe was an Oscar, and Sally was definitely a Felix. But their laughter stopped when their very different behaviors threatened their relationship.

Sally could not tolerate Joe's slovenly behavior. His clothes were strewn about the apartment, his wet towels were left on the bathroom floor, he wouldn't put his clothes in the hamper or his dishes in the dishwasher, and his desk was so cluttered that the piles of paper sometimes collapsed from their own weight. Joe's habits drove Sally bonkers, and she expressed the same disappointment and the same arguments about his sloppiness repeatedly, but to no avail.

Joe just couldn't understand what all the fuss was all about. He felt that Sally's excessive neatness was making him very uncomfortable and nervous. He argued with her, saying that he couldn't relax for fear of something being out of place. He couldn't be spontaneous, and he felt that he had to be on guard all the time. Each thought the other's behavior was bad news, possibly neurotic. Each saw the other's behavior as indicating deep character flaws. The tension between them became very uncomfortable for both.

Their standoff lasted for eight months. Finally, they realized that the issue was not worth destroying their relationship for. They were smart enough to begin exercising their romantic intelligence to reverse the emotional toll this rift was costing them. Both were empathetic, and each of them understood the impact their attitudes and behaviors had on the other. When they began to talk—not to argue or defend—but to talk, they agreed that their differences were not bad versus good, or right versus wrong; they were not character flaws, only differences, nothing more.

They talked about what they felt, without angry accusations and name-calling. Each wanted to make the other happier and both realized they had to make some changes to save their relationship. To reach an agreed-upon halfway point, Joe made heroic efforts to pick up after himself more frequently, and Sally made a real effort to ignore some of Joe's sloppy behavior. The situation wasn't perfect, but it was better than it had been. Their love for each other was more important than what the house looked like. Both felt supported in making their difficult adjustments, so they did not become polarized and fixed in their thinking and behaviors. They felt secure enough within themselves to try to make these adjustments and all the other changes that followed.

These initial changes motivated them to express their flexibility in other areas. They understood that some issues were not important enough to fight over; others were. Ongoing resolutions of many problems brought them closer together. Joe spoke his mind freely and Sally was honest, but never brutally so. She never used honesty as a weapon; she used it to bring them closer together. Most importantly, they served as each other's mentor for their continual psychological and emotional growth. The growth that each experiences is the result of the love they have for each other. Sally and Joe are living their romantic intelligence.

Dealing with new and more challenging issues is an important part of emotional compatibility in a romantically intelligent relationship. You learn to use your romantic intelligence to break through barriers in your partnership. Each new resolution of a difficult problem, handled in a romantically intelligent way, serves as a template for more effective solutions for life's ongoing issues and problems. When your Romantic IQ is high like Sally and Joe's, you realize there is no such thing as the perfect couple. But you do know that you can apply your romantic intelligence within the framework of your imperfections and your partner's. You can make things better for each other, but you can never make them perfect.

Sometimes, it's difficult to know whether you are compatible with your partner or not. When you have many conflicts, disagreements, and misunderstandings, you may think at those times that you don't have much in common with your partner. You may begin to ask yourself whether you and your partner are compatible.

You might assume that frequent disagreements, not having your needs met by your partner, and communication breakdowns are sure signs of incompatibility. But that may not be the case. Many people tend to generalize from these kinds of problems, and they perpetuate the mind-set of incompatibility during the difficult periods in their relationships. They misconstrue bouts of unhappiness and frequent conflicts with their partners as a basic form of incompatibility.

All relationships have communication failures, disappointments, hurt, and pain, and such rough patches apply equally, and just about as frequently, to incompatible and compatible relationships. As a romantically intelligent person, you know this is true, and you work to problem-solve what can be changed in your relationship. Compatibility means that you are more compatible with your partner than incompatible, especially in regard to issues that relate to expectations, needs, ways of communicating, intimacy and love, sensitivity, thoughtfulness, generosity, values, and beliefs.

Impulse Control

With many of the issues and problems couples face, their initial emotional responses may be strongly reactive, if not dramatic, and potentially damaging to their relationship. However, when romantic intelligence is operating, impulse control and self-monitoring will take over while you are becoming aware not only of your anger or frustration, but also of your effect on your partner. You use your self-talk to calm yourself down and to curb your expressiveness. Consulting with yourself moderates your impulses and allows room for reasonable discussion and problem-solving.

Learning How to Fight: Jane and Victor

In the first couple of years that Jane and Victor were married, their relationship impulse control was much less effective than it is six years later. Jane used to do a lot of shouting and, as she remembers it, "I would threaten to leave him—I always kept one foot out the back door." They both remember a ten-hour fight driving from Maine to New York. It was a marathon shouting match conducted in the pouring rain with bad visibility and little sleep.

Jane said, "Neither of us was willing to take a breather, the fight just went on and on." When it happened, she had a great need to be heard, having just come out of a relationship where she had never voiced her opinions, and Victor was overcompensating for a former relationship in which he had never asserted himself. Their "drive from hell" was a battle to exorcise the emotional baggage from their past relationships.

Victor and Jane learned a lot from that fight. They learned they could have "the mother of all god-awful fights, and still stay together," and they learned they were meant to be together to resolve some of the issues that still come up for them. Now they take breaks and time-outs and have learned how to be aware of their own emotional needs and those of their partner. "We don't play Twenty Questions with each other, or try to guess what the other is thinking or feeling. We tell each other straight out, what's wrong—or right." They are able to identify who's up or down on any particular day. "I know he's upset," Jane says, "when he starts to yell at the cats." He knows something's wrong when she lowers her voice to its contralto range.

To be romantically intelligent means that you don't have to have things done your way all the time. It means you don't have to save face, insisting that you're right and your partner is wrong, for fear of appearing ignorant, stupid, or weak. When two people come together, usually they start with a strong sense of compatibility; their philosophies, values, beliefs, and so on, mesh; and they share hopes for a future they mostly agree upon. However, *living* with your partner may bring up emotional flashpoints that you were not aware of at the beginning of the relationship: issues that deal with décor and neatness, and issues related to money, family, past lovers, secrets, and so on.

Is Your Partner the Only One Who Gives Meaning to Your Life?

Rather than expecting a relationship to meet all of your emotional needs and anticipating that you and your partner will see eye-to-eye with each other on all fronts, as a romantically intelligent person you learn to strike a good balance between independent thought and activities, and interdependency with your partner. For a romantically intelligent person, compatibility means creating enough of your own life separate from your partner while sharing enough of your partner's life to make your relationship work. The trick is to create enough of an independent life and to have a sufficient number of emotional outlets so your primary relationship isn't overburdened by having to meet all of your needs.

Compatibility in relationship is the freedom to say and think what you want, not just agreeing more than disagreeing, or having more shared likes than dislikes. Ask yourself these questions: "Can I be myself in this relationship? Can I grow and change? Does my partner support me in my independent activities?" If you answer yes to these questions, then your compatibility quotient is very high and your romantic intelligence is flourishing.

Emotional Compatibility

Emotional compatibility is the most significant predictor of relationship success, for it involves trust, intimacy, emotional expressiveness, and emotional health. Matters of self-confidence and self-esteem, the ability to love and empathize, and the qualities of persistence and self-motivation contribute to your emotional maturity and compatibility potential. Your emotional maturity expresses itself when you can nurture and support your partner's growth and development without seeing it as a threat to your relationship; instead you view your support as a way of enriching the quality of your relationship.

When two people allow each other to grow and change in their relationship, their connection becomes stronger, deeper, and more meaningful. However, if only one of you believes this model is workable and the other doesn't believe it, or "get it," you will experience compatibility difficulties, because you both bring to the relationship the different experiences that shaped your values and beliefs.

The amount of emotional support you experienced while growing up also will govern your expectations for your relationship, your rules for relating, and the responsibilities that you have to each other. If emotional support was lacking when you were a child, you may expect your partner to make up for what your parents didn't give you when you were growing up. Reassurances that you are loved and cared for may not convince you, because no matter what your partner says or does to support you, you may never be convinced of it. Compatibility in this scenario doesn't depend on communication issues, as important as they are, but on how you manage and work with your emotional states within the relationship.

Emotional Maturity Levels

People with similar levels of emotional maturity are usually attracted to each other. High-level emotionally mature people attract other high-level emotionally mature people. Similarly, low-level emotionally mature people attract other low-level emotionally mature people. The more emotionally mature you are, the fewer your "togetherness" needs will be.

The romantically successful relationship starts with the understanding that your happiness and personal fulfillment begin with you, not with your partner. To be romantically intelligent is to know that you are ultimately responsible for your own happiness. When your partner feels the same way, then you experience greater compatibility. If you experience a significant difference in this regard, then your sense of compatibility with your partner suffers. Emotional compatibility is grounded in emotional self-awareness. It requires you to be able to sense, read, and understand your own emotional states and signals. As a romantically intelligent person you take responsibility for your emotions. If you don't understand your emotional self you cannot understand your partner's emotional self.

EXERCISE: COMPATIBILITY CHECKLIST

If you are thinking about committing to a relationship, or you are in a relationship now, the following checklist will help you to think about the beliefs, expectations, and lifestyle issues that come up in all romantic relationships. Check off how many issues you and your partner have looked at alone or together.

My partner and I have discussed

_____ Our expectations of how things should work in a relationship (i.e., chores, finances and family obligations).

_____ Our social differences (whether we are both very social, or whether one of us is more or less introverted or extroverted than the other). We know whether we prefer group activities, small dinner parties, a heavy social life, or solitary activities.

____ Our sexual preferences (the kinds of sexual expressions we enjoy or would rather stay away from, our views on infidelity, and how we define the meaning of the term).

____ Our attitudes toward relationships outside of our couple bond.

____ Our lifestyles (personal habits, neatness or sloppiness).

____ What money means to us (our relation to money in the past and our present relation to it).

My partner and I have shared

____ The same goals, dreams, and vision of what we want to accomplish at various times in our lives, both as a couple and as individuals.

____ Our religious and ethical views, particularly the issues that cause us to become passionate.

____ How much time we need to spend alone as individuals and how much time we want to spend together.

____ Our feelings about having (or raising) children, and our attitudes toward our families.

____ Our attitudes toward past lovers and former relationships. Are these out-of-bounds and off the table for discussion, or are you either of you friendly with your ex?

____ Our feelings about secrets (do you believe in telling each other everything, or are some things best left alone?)

You can be in love with someone and not know anything about him or her. In the throes of passion, you don't think about issues that seem peripheral to your romance. But once the true reality of the person appears, you may discover that you can't tolerate his attitudes toward other people, or you are amazed that she holds those views. The more you know about your partner and the more he or she knows about you, the fewer the surprises, the less areas there are for conflict, and the greater your chance of building a foundation based on honesty and trust.

Disagreements and Conflicts

To be romantically compatible is to understand that conflicts are unavoidable to the success, health, and vibrancy of your relationship. Nonetheless, if you start to feel that you must distance yourself from your partner to protect yourself from continual, ongoing conflict, you should do so, because too many conflicts can overload your relationship and break it apart.

Too little conflict in a relationship, where one (or both) partners avoid arguments or deny any problems exist, creates a phony, dishonest, and insincere relationship in which lovey-dovey behavior covers up long-standing resentments and dissatisfactions. Remember, the romantically intelligent couple prizes honesty with each other to keep their relationship vital and alive. When dishonesty is present, resentment and anger build, and if these emotions are ignored, the relationship loses its emotional charge; indifference sets in and the relationship dies.

Romantically compatible couples agree on how conflict is used, expressed, and managed in their relationship. They understand that the way they handle and process their conflicts determines whether their arguments will lead to solving problems, greater intimacy, and personal growth for both, or whether the relationship will disintegrate into apathy and finally dissolution.

Conflict resolution and problem-solving for the romantically compatible couple involve talking about the issues that relate to spending habits, time together, intimacy, friendships, household chores, and child-rearing, among other thorny issues and problems. The couple with high Romantic IQs tries to avoid destructive criticism when they quarrel. They do not belittle each other's shortcomings, or call names, or strike emotionally vulnerable, sensitive spots. Destructive criticism, according to Goleman (1997) and others, is one of the most accurate predictors of marital breakdowns. Where complete alienation and disaffection have occurred, destructive criticism was likely to be the culprit.

Is Your Partner's Emotional Maturity Comparable to Yours?

Increasing your romantic intelligence requires increasing your emotional maturity. The ability to balance your own needs with your partner's, to value, support, and care for your partner's growth and freedom as much as your own, are the markers of emotional maturity in a relationship. Emotional maturity is the ability to sense what it is you feel and what it is your partner feels at any given time; it includes the ability to focus your emotional attention on your partner, making him or her feel loved, important, and supported.

Although emotional maturity in an individual is being authentic, honest, and comfortable with yourself, emotional maturity in a relationship requires you to think and act in the best interests of your relationship. You don't always think of your own interests first, and you don't automatically think of your partner's interests first because your motivation is to please him or her. You don't operate out of fear of disapproval, or fear of rejection, or fear that you'll lose the relationship. Emotional maturity requires time plus work. It involves understanding yourself better, working on your issues, and working with your partner to improve your relationship. It may also involve allowing your partner to be your toughest critic, if the critique comes from a place of love and concern, not belittlement.

The Bottomless Pit of Deficit Love

If your partner has not received adequate love, security, and support from her family, she may expect that her relationship with you will meet all the emotional needs that were never met by her parents. This kind of imbalance can put an unrealistic burden on your relationship, because no one person can make up for your partner's need for love and security.

Constantly reassuring your partner that you love her will not change her basic problem of feeling insecure and unloved in the first place. After a while, this situation will become tiresome and frustrating, because you will begin to feel that no matter how often you prove your love and support for your partner, it's never enough. Any independence, growth, or freedom you have may be seen as a threat to her. When you can't be yourself for fear that your partner will tell you that she feels unloved and unsupported, or if she tells you to play it safe by not taking a job promotion, or even not acquire new job skills, you will begin to feel suffocated by her. If you feel caged in and held back by your partner's restrictions, your good will, commitment, and caring for her will disappear. Stunting a partner's freedom to grow is not the sign of a romantically intelligent relationship, but the sign of one in trouble.

This form of emotional incompatibility, which is an issue of emotional maturity, causes relationships to self-destruct. Your partner's constant need for reassurance becomes a debilitating burden on your time, energy, and resources. You stop giving and start distancing, causing your partner to want even more emotional support than ever. When there is no longer any emotional vitality to the relationship, it drifts into apathy and indifference. If the emotional issues of the relationship are not addressed, the partnership reaches its conclusion, and finally ends.

If neither you nor your partner is experiencing emotional growth, there may be more of a preoccupation with your own needs being met, but little thought about meeting your partner's needs. There may be a strong egocentric orientation on both parts, with genuine caring, empathy, and altruism in very short supply.

In order to love someone, you must feel loved yourself. You cannot love in a romantically intelligent way without first loving yourself or feeling that you are worthy of love. If you feel secure within yourself, and you know who you are, you will have a strong identity; you will be morally and ethically autonomous, and you will know your likes and dislikes.

When you are romantically compatible, you learn to see being in a relationship as two separate individuals coming together to learn from each other and having the freedom to explore their possibilities, professionally, socially, emotionally, and psychologically. Emotional compatibility is a coming together to enrich each other's lives and to derive joy and satisfaction from the growth and freedom created by your union.

CHAPTER SEVEN

THE DANCE OF EMPATHY

[C]ompassion . . . signifies the maximal capacity of affective imagination, the art of emotional telepathy. In the hierarchy of sentiments, then, it is supreme.

—Milan Kundera
The Unbearable Lightness of Being

You have a friend who has just met someone special and is beginning to fall in love. Can you pick up on her news before she tells you about it? Have you ever detected someone's emotional distress just by sniffing the tension in the air around him? Can you "read" a blush, or scent the odor of illness descending on someone? Can you sense trouble coming in the next round of negotiations, even if the meeting seems to be going well and your brain is telling you otherwise? These skills—intuition, empathy, emotional literacy—are fundamental to expressing romantic intelligence and raising the level of emotional flow in your relationship.

Your own abilities in these areas may or may not be evident, but perhaps you know or have met someone who has this uncanny, almost psychic, ability to read thoughts and feelings. This person is so in touch with your emotional energy that she can tune into your feelings perfectly. She seems to know what's going on inside your mind, and can express what you are feeling. The explanation for her abilities lies in the dynamics of emotional empathy, the techniques of hypersensing and hypersight, expert listening, and the qualities that produce romantic flow.

What Is Empathy?

Empathy, the ability to intuit another person's moods and feelings on a pre- or nonverbal level, is an asset in all relationships, but is particularly desirable in romantic ones. The knack of reading feelings is especially crucial between partners in intimate relationships, because, as Daniel Goleman (1997) points out, "the emotional truth is in how [someone] says something rather than in what he says." Goleman goes on to suggest that "90 percent or more of an emotional message is nonverbal." That means you should pay attention to the way your partner communicates his message not only through his words but also through his tone of voice, facial expressions, eye movements, gestures, calmness or lack thereof, even his skin tone, and so on.

Some people are natural empathizers whose personalities and sensory mechanisms have developed acutely sensitive emotional radar that connects with and understands others, intuitively, at the feeling level. In his book *15 Steps to Impossible Dreams,* Steven Scott (1999) compares these individuals to golden retrievers (think of this breed's kind, empathetic faces). Such people are more likely to be givers than takers in most areas of their lives, and some of their generosity takes the form of being a good listener and lending a sympathetic ear.

Others, those who need to amplify their emotional intelligence and improve their social skills, can learn some of these techniques. There are people who have been so emotionally or psychologically abused that they must train themselves how to think about others, instead of thinking exclusively about themselves. As adults, once they have escaped from the pure survival mode of their past, they must practice thinking about others to expand their hearts and minds. There are still others, to be discussed near the end of this chapter, who are incapable of feeling empathic because they suffer from a personality disorder. Being able to identify these individuals is part of the skill of having emotional hypersight: that is, if you can gauge someone's empathy quotient, that will tell you a lot about that person.

The most literal example of empathic feeling is demonstrated when a husband experiences morning sickness or labor pains during his wife's pregnancy or delivery. So attuned to his wife's emotional and physiological state is he that his empathy extends to the biological level. This kind of biological "twinning" also occurs when a couple has been together for a very long time and they begin to resemble one another. Frances, who is both a wife and molecular biologist, understands the complexity of cell biology very well. She describes her marriage to her husband of twenty years this way: "My relationship with my partner is like biology—there's a level of granularity in it—we're so close, we know each other at the cellular level."

The Professional Empath

Empathetic powers depend on how attuned you are to your own emotions, how emotionally self-possessed and serene you are, and how well you read and interpret nonverbal language. There are some people who are so skilled at this that they can rightly be called "professional empaths."

Karla McLaren

Karla McLaren (2002), who refers to herself as an empath and emotional healer, describes the empathetic person in her set of tapes, *How to Become an Empath,* this way: "Empathic people have the ability to translate energetic impulses into emotional awareness. They feel their way through life, through decisions, and through relationships in a deepening and life-affirming way." Karla McLaren is an extraordinarily perceptive person and an experienced specialist who uses emotional intuition in her work with trauma patients to connect with them at a very deep and intense level.

A survivor of sexual abuse herself, McLaren is particularly interested in the phenomenon of dissociation, in which people, under conditions of tremendous stress or severe trauma, leave their bodies and pull their consciousness away from the situation, whatever it is, to avoid the psychic pain and emotional intensity of that moment. Those who used dissociation as a defensive mechanism over a long period of time have great difficulty getting back in touch with their feelings.

Carolyn Myss

Best-selling author and speaker Carolyn Myss calls herself a medical intuitive, someone who can pick up on the energies in the body and transform them into signs of physical and emotional health or illness. In *Anatomy of the Spirit,* Myss (1996) explains that her healing methods are based on "learning the language of the human energy system" and focusing particularly on the seven body centers or chakras that are basic to the philosophy of yoga. Working with her intuition, she has uncovered the emotional/spiritual causes of illness and has come to some striking conclusions about emotions and health.

Myss confirms the notion that the body sometimes "literalizes" psychic pain. For instance, her long-term practice provides evidence that people with heart disease shy away from love and intimacy; they actually block love from coming into their lives. This lack of love causes them to suffer from blocked arteries; their avoidance of emotional heartache becomes displaced into physical heartache, instead. Myss says that the same kind of dynamics are in play with cancer patients and those suffering from blood disorders. People with blood disorders, according to Myss, often have unresolved issues with their blood relatives, while cancer patients also present unresolved emotional issues, particularly with the past.

Claudia LeMarquand

A social worker and transpersonal therapist, Claudia LeMarquand looks at the layers of her clients' energies and emotions and gets "a general feel for how their insides are doing." LeMarquand defines intuition as "emotion raised to the level of thought." The more intuitive and thoughtful you become, she believes, the more you become congruent with the various parts of your self and integrated within yourself. She says, "There is something at the core that is clear."

LeMarquand views every relationship as a life lesson. She counsels: "When you're in relationship with someone else or if you choose a relationship with aloneness, you must ask yourself, 'What I am supposed to be learning from this experience?'" She has observed that some people are in relationships to learn how *not* to give themselves away. Others need to discover they don't always have to be "the warrior," while still others are learning that romantic relationships are a bona fide path to happiness.

♥

Consummate empaths like McLaren, Myss, and LeMarquand use their intuitive powers to understand and help people live healthy and emotionally harmonious lives. Although most of you won't become professional empaths, you can learn to strengthen your own intuitive skills and emotional literacy to enhance your empathetic powers and energize your relationship.

The Romantically Empathic Person's Characteristics

Although it is well-known that women are better than men at reading nonverbal cues, both sexes can improve their empathic skills to function better in their relationships. Some men seem to be natural empaths. For example, Karen thinks she fell in love with Dan when she got to know him at work. He is a video store manager, outgoing, warm, and skilled at reading people. He gently motivates his employees to suggest films and interact with their customers. "I loved the way Dan could read other peoples' feelings, and inspire us to do our best work," she said. Karen is impressed with how Dan picks up on his clerks' moods. On bad days, he literally changes the atmosphere of the whole store just by interacting with his employees and being receptive to their emotional states.

EXERCISE: TEST YOUR ROMANTIC EMPATHY

The following exercise will help you to determine your level of romantic empathy. In the space at the left of each sentence, write the letter "U," if you usually agree with the statement. If you sometimes agree, write an "S." If you never agree, write an "N." The more U's you put down, the more romantic empathy you have and routinely express. If there are no U's in your column, read on. You will need to work on developing the skills of romantic empathy.

_____ I am fascinated with the world of emotions.

_____ I try to be sensitive to my partner's feelings.

_____ I can pick up on and figure out the feelings behind my partner's words.

_____ I am good at spotting my partner's mood shifts and subtle emotional changes.

_____ I make myself available to talk and listen to my partner.

_____ I try to be balanced and noncritical when listening to what my partner says, and I try not to interrupt him or her.

_____ Even if I don't agree with my partner's attitudes or actions, I try to figure out where he or she is coming from.

_____ My partner and I spend a lot of time talking with each other.

_____ I am a warm and supportive partner.

_____ I try to walk in my partner's shoes.

Romantic empathy, like empathy at work or with your children and friends, is the ability to enter into another's world of feelings. It's the power of understanding and the ability to create harmonious, mutually engaged relationships. Romantically empathetic people have a strong drive to communicate with their partner and to connect with him or her at a deep emotional level. What does this mean in practical terms?

It means that issues and problems get talked through, and that feelings and emotions are acknowledged and heard. These relationships are lighthearted but not superficial: there is no pretense; there is trust. There is giving and mutuality, and, in general, a generous and altruistic spirit permeates the relationship. Partners are not slaves within the relationship, nor are they slaves to it.

Romantic Flow and Mirroring

At the beginning of a relationship, you and your partner are probably intent on establishing physical and emotional rapport. You both listen intently to what the other has to say, sometimes hanging on to every word, so you can remember it. Your chemistry, your mutual likes and dislikes, also draw you together and create rapport. For instance, Jack said he was instantly attracted to Judy because "She reminded me so much of myself." In fact, when two people are like each other, they tend to like each other.

When two lovers meet, they tend to tune into each other's flow and rhythm. *Mirroring* means getting into rhythm with your partner on as many levels as possible. When you mirror someone, that means you talk in similar ways, you sit the way she sits, you make love the way he makes love. When you mirror your partner, you are reflecting his or her energy, mind, and spirit. The degree of rapport that you establish with your partner, throughout your relationship, depends in part on your ability to mirror his or her emotional tone, your body language and listening styles, and shared values and beliefs.

Empathy also contributes to "romantic flow," which like the "flow" experience, generally takes place while running, writing, talking, or making love. Flow and complete rapport make you feel out of time; you live in the present moment, worry-free, attuned to yourself, your partner, or your creativity. The flow that manifests in relationship results in experiencing your partner for who she or he *is*, without any fantasy projections. When there is flow, there is a clear channel of communication, a sense of serenity and trust that permits the emotional energies of love, tenderness, and affection to open and be freely shared by each partner. Romantic flow permits comfortable, serene silences, too; you can be happy together even when neither of you has much to say.

Emotional Mirroring

If your partner feels blue and you approach her with an enthusiastic, backslapping, "Hey, how ya doing today?" you will be emotionally out of sync, and your romantic flow will be disrupted. Your partner will resent your insensitivity and being so out of touch with what she's feeling. You can understand this. You undoubtedly have had comparable experiences. There must have been times when you wanted to be by yourself to read or listen to music, and you couldn't, because your partner burst in, all jazzed up and ready for a heart-to-heart. The last thing you wanted was to talk or argue; what you did want was for him or her to back off and leave you to your tea and your "alone time."

To avoid the problem of being out of sync with your partner, it's essential to be sensitive to what she is feeling, and then act accordingly. If she seems blue, don't try to cheer her up with good-humored jokes. Instead, say something like, "Hon, it looks like you're really down in the dumps right now, would you like to tell me what's going on?" Such a question validates her feelings and conveys the message that you are listening, caring, and sensitive to her emotional state. It also encourages her to be more forthcoming about what is bringing her down. This doesn't mean that your partner is seeking a solution to whatever is on her mind; it does mean that she'll be able to talk about what's bothering her, because she'll see how sensitive you are to her mood.

Posture, Facial, and Gesture Mirroring

Your facial expressions, the way you look at your partner and make eye contact with him or her, your posture, where you place your hands, how you stand, even the way you breathe, all signal your emotional state to your partner. If he folds his hands across his stomach, for instance, what is he telling you about his emotional state? There is no right or wrong answer to that question, except that he seems to be putting up a barrier, or trying to be self-protective in a subliminal way. The more attuned you are to your partner's feelings, the more you can make sense of what his expressions and movements mean. However, reading body language is not always enough.

To avoid misunderstandings, no matter what you pick up from nonverbal cues, you also need to connect with your partner verbally. For example, you might say, "You seem upset. Is there anything bothering you? I'd really like to hear what you have to say." This second step is to make sure that you are reading him or her correctly, because body language can be misunderstood. In the example above where your partner folds his hands across his stomach, the interpretation might be right: he may be doing that as a distancing mechanism or to set up an unconscious barrier. However, it's also possible that folding his hands across his stomach signals he has an upset stomach or wants to warm his hands. Always confirm, never assume.

EXERCISE: MIRROR YOUR PARTNER'S BODY LANGUAGE

Daniel Goleman (1997) points to work by Robert Levenson, a University of California at Berkeley researcher, who has examined the physiology of emotional rapport in marriage and demonstrated that a spouse who mirrors his or her partner's body language and facial styles eventually establishes rapport to the point where both partners exhibit the same pulse rate and blood pressure numbers. Body mirroring can be thought of as reflecting your partner's body language back to him or her.

Note: Be aware that a lot of body mirroring is done from the chin up, for example, with a particular tilt of the head, or the certain way a hand is placed on the chin. Also, no one should try to do body mirroring in a "monkey see, monkey do" kind of way. Deliberate, outright mimicking would look ridiculous, probably insult your partner, and defeat the purpose of achieving emotional rapport.

Experiment with the techniques of body mirroring and record what happens in your journal. Be as subtle as you can. If possible, don't tell your partner what you're doing until you've completed this exercise at least five times and have noted his or her reactions.

Here's how to do it: If your partner crosses his or her arms, then you cross your legs or your ankles. If he rests his head in his hands, then you touch your chin. If his hands are in his pockets, try putting your hands in your pockets or folding your hands in your lap. Obviously, outright mimicking of your partner's body language shouldn't be overdone. But, done subtly, this exercise can help you to build greater rapport and emotional harmony with your partner.

Reading Emotional Tone: The Feelings behind the Words

Adjusting the tone of your voice and the tempo of your speech is another way to deepen your rapport with your partner. Tone and tempo refer to *how* you speak; not what you say, but the way you say it. Most of the information of a message is conveyed by how you say the words. It's in your loudness (or softness), inflection, tenor, and rhythm. Both the normal rate of speed and the normal decibel level differ in different cultures. Most people speak at a pace that allows them to enjoy listening to themselves. Pay attention to the speed and the tone of your partner's speech. Rapid speech may indicate excitement, nervousness, or anxiety. Slowed-down speech or a halting or erratic tempo can mean someone's really upset or angry. Well-modulated speech indicates confidence and self-possession.

Mirroring Values and Beliefs

Mirroring your partner's values and beliefs means that you do not denigrate, ridicule, or otherwise insult those values and beliefs, especially when they differ from yours. You listen and try to understand and make sense of what he or she says. You do not jump to conclusions. Moreover, if you don't agree with what your partner says, you are never abruptly dismissive; neither do you agree for the sake of keeping the peace.

Try to avoid using the word "no" before you make a statement or give an answer, and shy away from using "but" because it can negate everything you said before it. For example, don't say, "No, I really like the film." When you say, "You look really good today, *but* I don't really like those shoes," you undercut the effect of the compliment by being brutally honest. Often, your partner will hear only the negative part of the comment. It's also a good idea to avoid asking your partner too many questions, because he or she may feel that he is getting the third degree. Making declarative statements demonstrates that you know your own mind and you know how to speak it. If you do not speak your mind and confine yourself to asking questions, that diminishes your power as an equal partner. The best way to establish rapport is not to take exception or be argumentative just for argument's sake.

Share Problems

Sharing problems and solving them together can be an extremely strong relationship-builder, and a sign of your romantic intelligence. Keeping problems to yourself only creates distance from your partner, who will notice this. Relationship problems usually involve money management, personal habits that irritate one partner, issues about intimacy, trust, and commitment, illness, problems with in-laws or other relatives, child-rearing practices, difficulties at work, fallout with friends, and so on.

Empathetic, Nondefensive Listening

Listening is an art, a skill, and a discipline. Listening to your partner is all of those *doubled*, and, as with any other discipline, you can learn how to listen effectively. First, you need to know the fundamentals, what is involved in nondefensive listening. That is, you need to learn the essential techniques of silent attention, alert listening, and be able to express empathy after you've heard what was said.

Nondefensive, empathic listening takes place when you defer your own needs for a while to concentrate your attention on your partner while she is speaking. You need to learn how to listen to your partner and what to look for in nonverbal cues, facial expressions, body postures, and voice tones. Hearing becomes listening only when you give your full attention to what is being said and to how it is said.

Note: When you really listen, you are certainly not thinking about what you are going to say next or how you will respond. While your partner is still speaking, you are still listening. There is nothing more disheartening than trying to tell your partner something important, only to discover that he is only hearing you, not listening to you at all.

You show that you're listening to your partner by:

★ Your receptive body language

★ Paraphrasing his or her words

★ Asking for clarification

★ Making eye contact

★ Nodding your head attentively

★ Leaning toward your partner

You listen to your partner in order to

★ Show your support and to help your partner to express his or her feelings

★ Demonstrate that you are open to what she or he has to say

★ Enable each of you to speak and be heard

★ Be able to ask questions for clarification

★ Check assumptions

★ Clear up misperceptions and misunderstandings

★ Restate or paraphrase something your partner has said

★ Provide the silence necessary to encourage speech

★ Know when to bring to closure to your discussion and when to negotiate for agreement

You show your partner that you're listening when you

★ Listen without interrupting

★ Pay attention

★ Use supportive body language

★ Paraphrase feelings and observations

The following skills are good ways to respond, and will help your partner to understand what you care about, how you think about things, and where you're coming from:

★ Ask probing questions and ask for clarifications, like "What do you mean by that?" If you're not clear about what your partner has said to you, ask again.

★ Restate what your partner has said, capturing the essence but recasting it in a positive way.

★ Edit out sarcasm or highly charged phrases of language.

★ Try to always use "I" language instead of "You." Not: "When you do that. . . , you make me feel. . . ." Instead say, "When you do that I feel. . . ." Take responsibility for your own feelings. That will make your partner less defensive.

★ Be very clear and very direct with your partner. Make sure you are not being misunderstood. Ask your partner what he or she thinks about what you've just said, so that you can be sure your message was heard correctly.

When you pay rapt attention without talking or interrupting, this allows your partner to let off steam and clear his head. He'll thank you for it later. You also need to let your partner know that you understand when he feels strongly about something. You make your partner feel visible, both seen and heard, when he speaks to you about something important to him, and you give him your undivided attention. For deep rapport, you both must acknowledge and even experience your strong emotions. You can even encourage your partner to vent his feelings, and let him know you understand, by using such romantically intelligent phrases as, "I see what you mean." "I understand what you're saying." "You're making a good point." "I can see that you feel strongly about that." "I can understand how you could see it like that."

Active listening and good responding skills are not taught in school or college. They should be. These techniques are not hard to learn, but they do take practice. At first, improving your listening and responding skills may feel uncomfortable, unnatural, or even phony; but with practice they will become second nature to you. Practice these skills with your partner, your friends and colleagues, and your children. Your communication skills and your romantic intelligence will improve.

Partners with Little or No Empathy

The listening and responding skills described above will work with a partner whose emotions and personality fall within the broad normal range. But you may be with someone who uses his intuitive powers against you to undermine your self-confidence. What can you do if you are with someone who is emotionally manipulative, darkly intuitive, estranged from his own feelings, and inconsiderate of yours?

Alexithymics

Daniel Goleman (1997) calls the person without empathy "the man without feelings." This is someone who suffers from a condition psychiatrists have named *alexithymia*. The term describes a person whose inner life is flat or nonexistent. The condition is believed to have its source in a physiological problem. You should be aware (and this is part of hypersight awareness) that there are some people who are so self-involved, they lack any trace of empathy and use others only for their selfish ends. They do not understand their own emotions or those of others. If you see these qualities in your prospective partner, you should be aware that such problems are sometimes caused by physical issues and sometimes they are deep-seated psychological problems that are difficult, if not impossible, to treat, such as narcissistic disorders.

Alexithymics can feel emotions; they just don't express them or know what they're feeling. "What's more," Goleman says, "they have trouble discriminating among emotions as well as between emotion and bodily sensation" (1997, p. 50). Consequently, they present themselves to doctors complaining of physical ailments, when actually they are experiencing psychological and emotional distress. The alexithymic person has difficulties with emotional language and orientation, but someone with a severe narcissistic personality disorder completely lacks the ability to empathize with others or to show compassion at all. Alexithymics are incapable of feeling anything, sociopaths or psychopaths are incapable of empathy.

Sociopaths

There are degrees of narcissism across a wide spectrum of types but the most extreme form of narcissism is psychopathy. The sociopath or psychopath isn't necessarily a child molester or a serial killer. Sociopaths come from all walks of life, from all classes and professions. These are the people who never take responsibility for their actions and are never motivated to create a romantically intelligent relationship. They have very low Romantic IQs. All of their relationships are manipulative and exploitive and exist only to serve their own ends.

The distinguishing characteristics of these individuals are that they are extremely charming and emotionally and psychologically manipulative. They are exploitive, cunning, glib. They even may appear to be capable of empathy and deep feeling, but it is all an act. After squeezing someone's energies and assets dry, they will discard that person like a used lemon and go on to their next victim. Ironically, many narcissists have a well-developed form of psychic radar that identifies and hones in on others' soft spots and vulnerabilities very quickly.

The importance of being able to spot a sociopath is to guard against them, protect yourself, and get away from them as soon as possible. People with high Romantic IQs don't have relationships with those who suffer from these disorders, and if they do, it's a very short-lived friendship. Unfortunately, people with low Romantic IQs frequently fall victim to these predators, because sociopaths appeal to their need for approval. They act the part of the perfect partner and, when they gain their victims' confidence, they exploit them emotionally, socially, and especially financially, without mercy.

Hypersight and Empathy

Developing your empathic skills and your awareness of others is the key to developing your romantic intelligence. Empathy and awareness must be used judiciously and deliberately, so you do not bestow the gift of your friendship on someone unworthy of your warmth and kindness. That's why it's crucial always to look closer and see what a potential partner is really all about. Make mental notes, check out what doesn't feel right, use your intuitive powers to protect your emotional health and avoid needless hurt. Do not allow others to use your empathy as a way of taking advantage of you by appealing to your openness. Increasing your own self-awareness will ensure that you see right through the facades of those who are not right for you.

For example, Dottie, an administrative assistant and avid tennis player, always tests potential romantic partners on the tennis court. She said, "How someone acts on the tennis court reveals everything about his character, anger-management abilities, courtesy and thoughtfulness, and his sexist or nonsexist attitudes." Her partner Jeff passed the test with flying colors because he played hard and fought a good fight, without letting her win.

Rene, a warm sympathetic real estate agent, wasn't as successful. Without taking a really good look at Ted, and relying on completely on his charm and their great sex life, she married him after dating for eight months. Three years later, he had eaten up all her assets, mortgaged her house, and left her destitute. Had Rene done her homework, she would have known that Ted made a habit of running through his wives' assets before leaving them. Hypersight, looking closer, and becoming aware of Ted's manipulations might have saved her psyche and her possessions.

Emotional literacy and the ongoing dance of empathy in a relationship involves being able to read another's character and intentions, learning to pick up on someone else's moods and internal states, and the ability to send positive and powerful emotional signals yourself—what Daniel Goleman calls "driving" the emotional content of your relationship in mutually empowering directions.

CHAPTER EIGHT

EMOTIONS AND INTIMACY

*Why are we so able to discuss orgasm and so
unable to discuss our deepest feelings, emotions,
dreams, hopes and aspirations?*
—Michael F. Shaughnessey
Sexual Intimacy and Emotional Intimacy

Some would say that all relationships have an erotic or sexual dimension and that you will naturally gravitate to those you find appealing on many levels, including the erotic. When you like someone, even platonically, there is always a small spark of sexual tension or physical appeal involved. That's one of the many reasons emotional and sexual intimacy are so frequently tied together.

Do you confuse sexual intimacy with emotional intimacy and affectionate bonding? For many people, affection, emotional intimacy, and sexual intimacy are presumed to go together, as if intimacy and sex always accompany each other, and as if affection and emotional intimacy are possible only in the context of romantic relationships. Neither one of these suppositions is true. It *is* possible to have sex with someone without being intimate emotionally, and it is also possible to be emotionally intimate with someone with whom you do not have a sexual relationship. To say "I desire you" is not at all the same as saying "I love you."

As you will recall from chapter 2, when you have intense sexual intimacy without emotional intimacy, that is infatuation. When you have emotional intimacy, sexual intimacy, and affection, you have romantically intelligent love. Neither an intense infatuation nor a blind devotion, romantically intelligent love is a commitment to your partner in which an emotional space is created that fosters your sexual and emotional intimacy as a couple, a space that gives each of you room for other affectionate friendships.

The woman or man who cultivates various kinds of intimate relationships with other people, i.e., with her or his adult children or other family members, friends, colleagues, Internet buddies, and so on, diffuses any buildup of toxic emotions with his or her partner by removing some of the emotional pressure from their significant relationship. When you have other people to talk to about intimate issues, in addition to your significant other, you can learn a lot without feeling pressured.

Love and Sex

In the last few decades, American culture has not only pushed the envelope on sex, it has also opened it and shaken out all the envelope's contents. Sexual intimacy in America has gone public. The new openness that has taken sex out of private bedrooms and onto the airwaves allows us to talk more openly about it, obtain greater sexual satisfaction, and deal directly with sexual dysfunction in both sexes.

Although many bemoan the new explicitness as a moral breakdown and view modern American culture as equivalent to Rome at its most decadent, others see the sexual revolution as America still emerging from its Puritan past. This revolution has its roots in the 1920s, after the First World War. But not until the contraceptive pill was invented in the 1960s, did it really take root. Once women had control over their fertility, there was no turning back. According to Professor Michael F. Shaughnessey, the problems with this situation arise because students are taught how to have sex but *not* how to love. He asserts that both in the culture at large and in American education, there is a fundamental dichotomy in the way that Americans approach intimacy.

> In high schools, students are taught about their reproductive organs and how to prevent pregnancy but they are not taught anything about how to communicate their feelings, or how to nurture emotional intimacy. Condoms are available in bathrooms, but learning how to say "I love you" remains a mystery for some. For others, those words are expressed solely to gain sexual favors and have no deeper meaning (1988).

Professor Shaughnessey has a point. Sex education classes, books, and manuals, R- and X-rated movies, the Internet, talk shows, condom dispensers, magazines, TV, the Starr Report, every aspect of human sexual functioning, every personal proclivity or practice, and every disease you can imagine have all been made abundantly explicit. But only recently with the publication of such books as *Emotional Intelligence* (Goleman 1997) and its offshoots, have many of us realized that teenagers and adults need instruction in the art of emotional intimacy as much as—or more than—they need instruction in sexual functioning.

What Is Sexual Intimacy?

Sexual intimacy can be the ultimate expression of romantic love or it can be the cold-hearted exchange between a sex worker and a lonely traveler seeking sexual gratification. Sexual intimacy refers to a spectrum of activities from holding hands, to touching, kissing, and hugging, and to other sexual behaviors that may result in sexual arousal, pleasure, and orgasm. Partners engaged in sexual intimacy may have known each other for many years and be familiar with every nuance of each other's erotic preferences. Or they may have met at a bar just a few hours ago. People seeking sexual intimacy may be teens exploring their sexuality for the first time, or they may be long-ago lovers who met each other again after their spouses have passed on.

The innumerable sexual encounters taking place daily may be mutually satisfying, one-sided pleasure, violent, anonymous, full of nervous timidity, or brimming with ease and laughter. Sexual intimacy can take place over the phone, in cyberspace, and may or may not involve verbal communication. Practiced lovers may communicate directly with their partner, explaining preferences, needs, desires, and feelings that will be incorporated into their lovemaking; or they may make love in silence, having talked through their preferences in advance. Other couples are more inhibited and find it difficult or impossible to discuss their fantasies and desires.

Authentic and Inauthentic Sexuality

The emotionally and romantically intelligent person is sensual, sexually communicative, and open to the full range of sensations his or her senses and body can provide. She can say "no" when she chooses to, and he is clear about what he needs to satisfy himself. Generous and candid with her partner, she does not playact during sex, but sees genuine lovemaking as the physical expression of her emotional intelligence. His sensuality is fluid and flexible, because he doesn't rely on the prescribed roles and rules touted by magazines, TV, and movies.

In other words, the woman with a high Romantic IQ doesn't flaunt her sexuality, or cater to a man to please him; she prefers to explore a mutually satisfying sex life with her partner. Her lovemaking is spontaneous and natural, not artificial or forced. She doesn't lose her self-respect in sex and preserves her singular identity. As with other kinds of emotional expression, she is clear, direct, and focused with her lover. She pays attention to her lover's needs as well as to her own. Most importantly, she is willing to discuss sexual problems with her partner in a straightforward and empathetic way. Because she keeps herself informed about sex and relationship issues, she doesn't shy away from problems but chooses to solve them, together with her partner.

Do You Sexualize All of Your Relationships with the Opposite Sex?

The culture, the media, some parents, and other authority figures socialize boys and men to objectify and sexualize all girls and women. Evolutionary psychological theory reinforces these influences by asserting that men are biologically programmed to respond sexually to all women, to perpetuate the human race. But when a man sizes up every woman he meets as a potential mate, he cuts himself off from the possibility of other kinds of relationships with women, such as friend, colleague, mentor, and student.

There are also women who, because they were socialized to jump to certain sexual conclusions, sexualize any attention, friendliness, or affection they receive from a man; that is, they are emotionally needy. Or they may have been sexually abused or molested as girls. Girls and women who have experienced any kind of sexual abuse, even "mild abuse," such as being raised by a seductive father, also tend to equate any sexual attention with love. Lisa, a New York City publicist who was raised by a seductive father, says that every man with whom she comes in contact, whether he's a boss, a colleague, a friend's husband, is automatically classified in the sexualized category.

When you sexualize gestures of genuine friendship and exaggerate casual relationships as romantic possibilities, you create assumptions and set up certain expectations. This revs up your fantasy-making programs and sets you up for major disappointment. The following story presents a sad account of how this works.

Jim and Melissa

Melissa always sat next to Jim at church. Both young people were single, and he was a friendly, sympathetic listener who clearly enjoyed their companionable talks before and after services. However, they never saw each other outside of church and rarely discussed their personal lives. Jim was in love with the woman he was dating and he viewed Melissa as a casual friend. But Melissa began to imagine that their church encounters were dates. She began to fantasize that, when the annual church trip came around, she would travel with Jim, and after dinner they would wind up together in his room. She spent a lot of time embroidering this fantasy. It made her feel very hopeful.

When the day of the church trip arrived, Melissa saw Jim get on the bus with his girlfriend. But she didn't allow herself to understand that he was involved with someone else. Only when they arrived at the hotel and he requested a double room did the reality begin to sink in and she became enraged. She could not restrain herself. She made an ugly scene at dinner and spent the rest of the evening crying in her room.

Clearly, by misreading Jim's attention and allowing her fantasies to rule her romantic life, Melissa set herself up for a humiliating experience and a grievous disappointment. This is not to say that it was all Melissa's fault—maybe Jim was the kind of guy whose friendliness comes across as "flirtiness." There are people of both sexes who require constant reinforcement of their sexual appeal. If they can conquer a woman or man with their looks or charm, that bolsters their ego, and they feel they've still "got it."

♥

Romantically intelligent people have a more nuanced view of their sexuality, and themselves. They rejoice in sexual pleasure but see it as only one aspect of their relationship, and as only one part of their total appeal as people. Their attractiveness comes from their emotional depth, ethical integrity, and erotic appeal. They understand themselves as having many dimensions, not only the sexual.

What Is Emotional Intimacy?

Basically, emotional intimacy is being up front about what you feel and what you think. When you are emotionally intimate with someone, you allow that person inside your private emotional space, because you feel it's safe for him or her to be there, because over time you have tested each other and have developed mutual trust.

Ironically, emotional intimacy begins by becoming intimate with yourself, by getting to know who you really are, and by taking the journey to self-awareness described in chapter 4. For the woman with romantic intelligence, knowing how her mind works, what her fantasies are, how her body works, and what gives her pleasure, are her keys to a rich sexual and emotional life. Such knowledge makes it possible to have a deeper, more meaningful, and more sustaining relationship with her lover.

Emotional intimacy comes about by sharing your deepest emotions and your innermost thoughts with your partner. Many couples "make love" in the course of their conversations, by listening and communicating matters of an exclusively private, personal nature. Disclosures in which you tell each other "everything" are the foundations of emotional intimacy. Clearly, sexual and emotional intimacy overlap in romantic relationships; they make up a couple's intimate dance.

Emotional Intimacy and Boundaries

In any intimate relationship, but especially a new one, your physical and emotional boundaries are always an issue. It's a question of whether you put up boundaries with your partner that are too strong and you never reveal yourself, or you have boundaries that are too porous, or even no boundaries at all, and you allow your identity to slip and merge with your partner's.

Your boundary issues also relate to how much intimacy you express, or don't, with your partner. Emotional intimacy stabilizes a relationship. Lack of emotional intimacy destabilizes and can even disintegrate a relationship. Lack of boundaries and unbalanced intimacy can threaten and weaken your identity.

EXERCISE: HOW DO YOU RATE ON INTIMACY ISSUES?

This exercise will help you gauge the level of intimacy you share with your partner. Mark a T for true and an F for false as appropriate.

When you have filled in your answers, go back and add up the number of Ts and Fs. What your scores indicate is explained below:

_____ I tell most of my secrets to my girlfriend.

_____ When I meet any man, I automatically check him out as a romantic partner.

_____ I often say to myself, "What my partner doesn't know won't hurt him."

_____ Some of my closest relationships are with gay men.

_____ I'm embarrassed to tell my partner what turns me on sexually.

_____ I don't tell my partner when I'm attracted to another person.

_____ I don't want my partner to tell me if he thinks someone else is attractive.

_____ I can be emotionally intimate with a woman in an instant, but when it comes to my partner I clam up.

_____ I always tend to lose myself in romantic relationships.

_____ I am having an Internet "affair."

_____ The most intimate emotional relationship I have is with a woman or man other than my partner.

The more Ts you have, the lower the intimacy level with your partner is and the more you rely on sources outside your relationship to meet your emotional needs. The more Fs you have, the higher the level of intimacy you enjoy with your partner. Although romantically intelligent women and men enjoy emotional intimacy with their close friends, counselors, mentors, and family members, if they are in a committed relationship, their primary source for emotional intimacy is their partner.

Intimacy and Emotional Risk

Emotional intimacy is a risky business, because it requires you to let down your guard and allow your partner to see your vulnerabilities and deepest secrets. Like a cat that exposes her throat after having learned over time to trust her human caregiver, you allow your partner to see your soft spots. You trust that he will accept you as a whole person, including your imperfections and flaws. You trust that he will value you for who you are and keep your confidences, hold your secrets close, and not judge you. You trust your partner's character and judgment not to betray your trust or to ridicule your dreams.

As you take small risks with someone, trust builds. When your partner takes risks, that will encourage you to disclose more and to take bigger emotional risks together. When you are both taking risks and exposing more of yourselves to each other, intimate knowledge and caring increase. In short, a romantically intelligent relationship allows you to feel comfortable and be yourself with your partner: you can speak your mind, you are honest and authentic, you feel loved and understood more often than not, and you and your partner can agree to disagree. You don't think to yourself: "What my partner doesn't know won't hurt him." You motivate each other and your problems are not shelved but dealt with in a timely manner.

Emotional Viagra

There are some couples that require emotional Viagra, that is, an infusion of emotional intimacy and passionate exchanges to build up the emotional dimension of their relationship. Emotionally arid, empty, expressionless relationships come about when you and your partner are not able to discuss your feelings, even though you are sexually intimate. You share a bed and have regular sex, but you keep your pain, sorrows, dreams, and hopes to yourselves. You never give expression to your deepest, innermost thoughts because the two of you find yourselves incapable of communicating feelings, thoughts, and aspirations. Relationships, though sexual, require emotional Viagra to grow and sustain themselves: without it you withdraw or look for emotional fulfillment in another direction.

In some relationships, there's more emotional sharing, mutual self-disclosure, and intimate communication than sexual intimacy. Some couples report that they stay up all night talking rather than making love. Optimally, your relationship incorporates both sexual and emotional intimacy. Of course, there are many reasons, which can include physical or medical conditions, that successful couples will have sporadic or even no sexual intimacy, but their emotional connection remains fulfilling and deepens with time.

Intimacy and Identity

Neither sexual intimacy nor emotional intimacy constitutes surrendering your identity as an expression of love for your partner. True expression of love for your partner occurs when you respect each other's boundaries and right to independence. When you are engaged with and committed to a sexual, emotional person with an intact and multifaceted identity—someone you may agree or disagree with and, at times, you may not understand—then you have achieved true romantic love. Then your relationship provides both freedom and security.

Today, in romantic relationships, there's a balance between roles and responsibilities that is more genderless than ever before. You are free to maintain your own friendships without being labeled an "emotional adulterer." You are free to have friendships with other men and women. A variety of complex relationships outside of your relationship with your significant other is acceptable to and encouraged by your partner. A friend of ours, an artist, puts the need for separate identities within a relationship this way: "When you merge too much, there's only one surface to the relationship and you sink to the lowest level of each other's neurosis. You need two surfaces to produces kinetic energy, power, and electricity."

Girlfriends and Emotional Intimacy

Most women have close friendships with other women and can establish intimacy quickly with women they don't know. After five minutes, many women who've never met before can talk frankly to each other about their divorces, their children's problems, their gynecologists, and their views on everything from hormone therapy to their partner's inability to communicate. Why do you think that women can meet each other on a plane or at a conference and cut through the conventions of conversation so quickly to arrive at emotional intimacy?

Perhaps it's because most women have been socialized to seek emotional intimacy outside of their primary relationship. Perhaps it's because those with less power in a culture talk more than those with more power. Women talk to other women easily because other women are not emotionally "other," as many men are "other." They are maternal substitutes or sister surrogates, and part of the sisterhood of talkers and confidantes. Instant intimacy and emotional rapport take place among women at beauty salons, in doctors' offices, at soccer games and school plays. Women understand that intimate relationships with other women meet their deep emotional needs. They nurture and cultivate these relationships because other women can be profound empathizers.

Emotional Infidelity

Emotional as opposed to sexual affairs have always been around, but they are probably facilitated and made more visible by the Internet and by women's increasingly interactive and powerful positions in their careers. There are many reasons for extrarelationship attachments. Suffice it to say that emotional affairs raise issues about the nature and character of fidelity in a relationship. They call attention to the issues of familiarity and lack of excitement that many long-term relationships have trouble with.

Emotional affairs happen when you are bored, you think you need a romantic fix, or when you can't spend time with your spouse. Someone comes into your life and you click, or he understands you, or he excites you in ways your partner doesn't. "Maybe your partner is a prude and you can't explore your sexual fantasies or express parts of yourself with him," says Pepper Schwartz, a University of Washington sociologist (Blumstein and Schwartz 1983). She goes on to say, "For people determined not to leave their existing relationships, an emotional affair is an attempt to reconcile conflicting needs."

An emotional affair can be instructive and reveal to you secrets about yourself and your hidden needs and desires, depending on the strength and character of your primary relationship. You can't generalize about or judge emotional affairs as bad or good—they are just a reality that intimate relationships encounter often and they can't be guarded against. You and your partner are not hothouse plants and you will naturally be attracted to others and be attractive to others. The best way to protect your relationship during an emotional affair is to strengthen your primary bond through mutual disclosure and emotional honesty. Being open and honest with your partner about what's happening and being clear about your priorities is your best insurance.

Online or Cyberspace Intimacy

John, who has witnessed the burgeoning of online intimacy and Internet affairs in his practice, calls this phenomenon, "the World Wide Web of imagination." Chat rooms and e-mail permit users to establish instant intimacy with strangers. In virtual reality, they let their imaginations run wild by creating false identities and having freaky sexual adventures. Chat room trysts, private and extensive e-mail communications, so-called cyber or virtual sex, are like having the cake and eating it, and not having the cake and not eating it.

There is a kind of intimacy generated during e-mail correspondence that is unique, anonymous, and intimate, all at once. An e-mail correspondence provides a space that encourages you to take emotional risks. It's quite different from a phone conversation were you can read someone's voice and hang up if you want to. Once you've clicked that mouse on "Send," though, you can't take back what you've said or where you've sent your message. Also, you have no control over the actions of the person to whom you've sent your mail

The phenomenon of online intimacy makes having intimate relationships with individuals from all over the world possible, and virtual sex or "cybering" a reality. This new form of bonding, the closeness that techno-intimacy induces, is producing new kinds of emotional and sexual intimacy. "Friendships, whether they are hatched over the Internet or in the flesh, begin and develop quickly when someone connects with a person who appears to be empathetic and who shares common interests," writes Shirley Glass, a Baltimore-area clinical psychologist who has cowritten *Infidelity on the Internet* (2001) with psychologist Marlene Maheu and therapist Rona Subotnik.

The romantically intelligent person is savvy about electronic intimacy, aware of the abuses of trust and pitfalls of online intimacy, and is careful not to give her secrets and trust away to anyone. Remember that with the click of a mouse, all of your private thoughts and intimate fantasies can be forwarded to anyone in the world. The implications of Internet affairs are staggering and their impact has not been thoroughly assessed in terms of effects on intimacy and relationships. The jury is still out and it will take another decade or so before the phenomenon can be assessed properly.

CHAPTER NINE

CONFLICT AND
EMOTIONAL CRISES

*The emotional health of a couple depends
on how well they air their grievances.*
—Daniel Goleman
Emotional Intelligence

As smart and as emotionally healthy as you and your partner may be, you both know you have limitations and shortcomings that are reflected in your conflicts. Even in the most romantically intelligent relationships, conflicts must and do occur. In this chapter, we hope that you will discover that dealing with your partner to correct misunderstandings can serve as a springboard to growth, greater awareness, and deeper intimacy. However, you must first understand that in order to feel and express the positive emotions of love, pleasure, and happiness with your partner, you must express your anger, frustration and disappointment, too.

If you deny or ignore your negative feelings for your partner, you will find that you cannot feel or express your positive feelings. The cardinal rule you both must honor at all times is this: To say what you feel in the moment, no matter how agitated or impassioned you may feel at that moment. That is how to use your romantic intelligence to resolve conflicts.

Conflict Resolution and Romantic Intelligence

If your relationship is strained, in trouble, or has ended, one or both of you is not applying your romantic intelligence. There may be a failure to face conflicts realistically and constructively, or a failure to cope effectively with the strains and difficulties of the conflict. Perhaps there isn't enough self-awareness. Perhaps you or your partner are not able to see the problem as a relationship responsibility, so you don't understand the importance of the issue you are quarreling about. (Or you didn't understand how important it was, until it was too late.)

Perhaps one of you was intent on finding fault and laying blame. Perhaps you insisted that your partner should change his or her ways while you remained blameless, insisting that the issue had nothing to do with you, only with your partner? If that was the case, then, basically, your attitude was, "So why change?" But that attitude cannot solve problems. The romantically intelligent approach to conflict means the following conditions exist:

1. You are in tune with your partner's emotions and with your own.

2. You understand exactly what you're feeling.

3. You interpret your feelings realistically, that is, you recognize your feelings as a message about what the problem is.

4. You decide whether the problem is important enough to discuss with your partner.

5. If the problem is important enough, you find the right time to address it with your partner.

6. You sort out and understand how much of the problem is caused by your partner, how much of it by you, and how much of it may be caused by your past.

7. You calm down or take a time-out if you are too upset with your partner before and during your conversation. Make sure that this condition is agreed upon as a ground rule before any discussions take place. It is important that you both use this technique as a form of damage control in your future discussions, too.

8. You are very clear and concise as you state your problem to your partner. For example say, "I am feeling very (e.g., angry) because of (e.g., the way you criticized me in front of our friends).

9. If you are the one to bring up the issue, offer a solution, too. If your partner brings up an issue with you, he or she should also offer a solution, to solve the problem effectively, if not quickly.

It would be great if you always knew exactly how to respond to all the troubling situations and miscommunications that come up in relationships. Most of us try to improve and get better at working through issues with our partners, but we are never perfect. Your own romantic intelligence tells you that not all issues can be solved. When you come to terms with this reality, you and your partner may even decide to live with a problem rather than have it drive a wedge between you.

Conflict Triggers

What common triggers set off conflicts? The list is extensive: Money and finances; parenting; problems with in-laws and other extended family members; sexual issues; intimacy and distancing issues; jealousy; power and control issues. These are powerful triggers that detonate emotional crises in relationships. Other equally powerful triggers include emotional and physical problems, addictions, feeling stuck in routines, becoming bored with yourself or your partner, too many responsibilities, aging, death, empty nest syndrome, retirement, and so forth—the list could even be longer. Your relationship's emotional equilibrium can be overthrown and turn toxic very quickly, unless you and your partner have the knowledge and skills to modulate and manage your feelings during arguments and conflicts.

The Consequences of Letting Go and the Pitfalls of Peacekeeping

Throughout this book we have stressed that your romantic intelligence involves tuning in to, feeling, and living a life of emotional vitality with your partner. We have said over and over again that you can use your emotions to promote your personal growth and the well-being and growth of your partner. We hope that you are relishing the intensity of joy, the warmth of sharing, and are learning even to welcome anger and disappointment.

It is equally important to understand that just letting go with your feelings, that is, allowing your emotions to spill out of you without thought and with little regard for the consequences—to your partner or to your relationship—is a recipe for disaster. It is not romantically intelligent to act impulsively, with little sensitivity to your partner's feelings. Remember, to be emotionally in tune is to have empathy for your partner and to have impulse control with yourself.

The old adage "think before you act" holds true if you want to live as a romantically intelligent person with a relationship that reflects this. Romantic intelligence is more than being able to feel and express your emotions; it is also about controlling them. Sadly, there are some people whose lives are so filled with intense, unregulated, and uncontrolled emotional experiences that they are proud of how emotional they are. They express irritation, frustration, and anger easily, with little or no provocation. Such people believe that being genuine and authentically human means to "let it all hang out," regardless of the consequences. Deep passion and clinging behaviors characterize the romantic and sexual parts of their relationship. They view it as honest and real, because it is so emotional and so focused on feelings. But they may have an emotionally excessive relationship.

Emotionally Excessive Relationships

Paradoxically, an emotionally excessive relationship is not necessarily caring or sensitive. It may be based on the need for reassurances, security, and undying devotion from your partner. This kind of emotionally overloaded relationship involves taking but not giving. The excessively emotional partner will try in vain to get self-love and self-esteem from her partner that she doesn't have in herself. In this kind of relationship, emotions are used to manipulate your partner to have things your way.

If you lack self-awareness and can't figure out why you feel what you are really feeling below the surface, you will readily express anger, frustration, sadness, or self-pity to cover up your true feelings, which may be fear of rejection and emotional pain, or a sense of worthlessness. Flamboyant emotionality can also mask your inability to generate your own happiness, which would require you to take the necessary steps to create a life of your own, a life where you would experience the rewards of your own accomplishments.

Managing Your Emotional Conflicts

You can manage your relationship only as well as you can manage your emotions. The strain of mismanaging your emotions will precipitate emotional crises for the two of you. In any relationship, your emotions are in partnership with your mind. The ability to make sense of what you feel is mediated by your thinking processes. Feelings that are expressed and experienced without thought create emotional imbalances that negatively affect your relationship with your partner and others.

EXERCISE: HOW DO YOU RESOLVE CONFLICT?

The following list of true and false statements will help you to see how you normally deal with conflicts in your relationships. Place a checkmark in front of a statement that describes your behavior during a conflict. When you have finished, go to the end of the exercise to determine how effective your actions are.

1. ____ During a conflict, I understand what I'm feeling.

2. ____ I bury issues and problems.

3. ____ I keep the peace at all costs.

4. ____ I take action to solve impasses with my partner.

5. ____ I tend to capitulate without solving a problem.

6. ____ I enjoy quarreling because it feels so exciting.

7. ____ I try to let some time pass after a fight before I deal with the issues.

8. ____ I express my hostility indirectly but I still "get back" at my partner.

9. ____ I habitually try to save face by claiming not to be angry.

10. ____ I face any real or imagined problem head-on.

11. ____ I distance myself from my partner and give him or her the silent treatment.

12. ____ I threaten to leave all the time when my partner is being difficult.

13. ____ When we fight, I start to overeat or I drink alcohol or smoke a joint.

14. ____ Anger and frustration at my partner drive me to the shopping mall.

If you checked off numbers 1, 4, 7, and 10, you take a romantically intelligent approach to arguments and conflict. If you checked any one of the others, you will need to work on modifying your approach to conflict, and then apply more direct and self-protective behaviors when you find yourself arguing with your partner or anyone else.

Does this list reveal that you turn frustration and anger inward by acting out in self-destructive ways? Do you use extramarital affairs, overeating, alcohol and drug abuse, compulsive shopping, dieting, gambling, depression, anxiety, and so forth to assuage your hurt feelings and anesthetize your difficult emotions? Do you have some sense of what your partner is feeling, too? Or do you use your upsetting emotions to feel bad for yourself as a way to exact revenge on your partner by quarrelling and threatening him or her with dreadful consequences?

Romantic intelligence is not only about feeling your emotions and expressing them appropriately, or feeling them and appropriately *not* expressing them, it is also about managing your emotions *during* your relationship difficulties. The romantically intelligent person turns toward his emotions, feels them, understands them, and then takes appropriate action. He doesn't use his emotions to justify himself or win a conflict with his partner where the issue becomes proving how right he is, rather than solving the problem. He uses his emotions constructively not destructively, in other words, he rechannels his emotions to empower himself rather than let them render him helpless.

Shutting Down or Converting Emotions

Emotions are always a part of you, whether you embrace them or ignore them. They are always active, sometimes hidden from self-awareness, other times very much in evidence. Strong emotions require you to be able to think about how to use their power and how to influence your circumstances to push through difficult logjams with your partner.

Shut down your emotions and they build up in your body and push you into addictive behaviors—too much smoking, drinking, or eating, too much socializing or overworking, too much drugging or other obsessive or addictive behaviors. The paradox is that the more you try to control your emotions or run away from them, the more control they have over you and how you feel. Emotions govern how you face your partner and what you do to yourself.

For example, if there are unresolved problems in your relationship because they are not acknowledged and never faced, the real issues remain hidden. You or your partner may manage the resulting stress, resentment, and unhappiness by releasing your tension in romantically unintelligent ways. Drinking, gambling, compulsive shopping, and clandestine affairs may make you feel good temporarily, but they spell disaster for your health and for your relationship.

Failing to communicate honestly with your partner may cause you to withdraw emotionally or explode at him with rage with little or no provocation. Furthermore, in many troubled relationships, a partner will convert hostility and anger into physical symptoms. "Conversions" like these transform emotional symptoms into physical ones in the unconscious effort to decrease the strength of the unexpressed emotions. This shift may reduce the negative emotional overload that your partner and you experience temporarily, but such patterns are strongly resistant to change, and they still don't address the primary issues.

If you want your relationship to heal and to rejuvenate itself, you must be honest with your partner. Lack of honesty will lock you both into repetitive, no-win arguments. Moreover, if you focus only on the symptoms, you will avoid the deeper issues that need to be addressed.

The Romantically Unintelligent Approach to Conflict

The following story is an example of low romantic intelligence. This story underscores the importance of tuning into your emotions, understanding what you're feeling, and finding the appropriate time to discuss what you're feeling with your partner. You cannot ignore or deny what you feel and simply expect everything will be fine. When you discuss your feelings, you're also telling yourself and your partner what your needs are, whether they arise from your relationship, your past, or something outside of your relationship. When you talk about your emotions, you start working on the issues, rather than allowing pain to build and accumulate. You cannot hold your partner responsible for any problems that exist between you because of your fear to speak your mind.

Barbara and Bill

Barbara and Bill married after dating for almost a year. He had fallen in love with her immediately; she was so confident and self-possessed, a young woman with a promising future. Secretly, he wondered why Barbara had chosen him from all the men she had dated, but he was happy that he was the one. Barbara loved Bill's kindness, generosity, and cheerful nature. Although she made more money than he did, it didn't matter. She loved him, so what he earned wasn't an issue. For nine years, Bill went to his job and supported his wife's career. They both thought they had a wonderful relationship with few problems, except for Bill's exceedingly high blood pressure.

Barbara was a smart, successful executive in a growing company. At thirty-three, she was on the fast track to even greater success with her organization. One day, her boss told her that she was in line for a promotion. She was slated to head her company's branch office in another state. Barbara was absolutely ecstatic when she heard the news. All of the hard work and the endless hours that she had put into her job had finally paid off. She couldn't wait to tell Bill. Driving home, she remembered how much his support had meant to her, especially during those long work days when she came home late at night. He had always waited up for her and supported everything that she had done to further her career.

When she got home, Bill didn't disappoint her. When she described her upcoming promotion and their need to relocate, he smiled and told her again how much he admired her and supported her rise up the corporate ladder. All Barbara could think about was how lucky she was to have Bill by her side—he was so supportive, so understanding, and so caring.

Then one day the unthinkable happened. She was dining late with Bill after a long day at the office and was telling him how excited she was, and how grateful she was for his support. As she was talking, she sensed something was wrong. Bill had a strange expression on his face, one she hadn't seen before. She dismissed his odd look, though, and continued talking. But then she saw that Bill's face was getting redder and his lips were twisting strangely. His body started to tremble, and suddenly he erupted in a rage, yelling at her at the top of his lungs.

"I can't take it any more. You're a selfish bitch who thinks only about your own needs. What about me, Barbara? Don't you think I need a life?" He kept repeating over and over how he couldn't "take it anymore." Finally, he stormed out of the room. Barbara stood still, transfixed and frightened by his emotional explosion. He had never yelled at her that way before. For the first time in her relationship with him, she felt frightened.

His explosion proved to be so destructive that neither one of them was able to recuperate from the experience. It changed their relationship forever. Shortly after, Bill moved out and Barbara was left to pick up the pieces of her shattered life alone. Her only contact with Bill was through his lawyer, when their marriage was put to rest in divorce court. In the years that followed, Barbara thought a lot about her "wonderful" relationship with Bill and wondered what had gone wrong. She reached the conclusion that Bill had never been honest with her. She thought that if he had only been able to say what he was really feeling, instead of being so hypocritical, they might still be together. He had preferred to keep a lid on all the anger and resentment that he felt, until he ran out of room for his buried feelings and they boiled over.

♥

If you're continually frustrated about what you don't receive from your partner, it is inevitable that your relationship will go into a crisis like Barbara and Bill's. You won't be able to get rid of the general malaise that never lightens, because you won't address your unhappiness by pointing inward at yourself. You will simply express your accumulating anger at your partner, always locating the reason for your troubles out there—in your partner, your friends, or your colleagues at work, never within yourself. Or you might become so preoccupied with what you're feeling and how unfairly you're being treated, that you will miss the signals that your partner sends to you about how frustrated she or he is with your attitude and behavior.

If you don't use your emotions and feelings to empower yourself to change something about yourself or your relationship, you will experience the opposite of what you feel, and you will hurt your relationship instead of helping it. You will use your anger, frustration, disappointment, or sadness to get even with your partner for not meeting your needs, whether real or imagined. If the behavior persists, it's a sure sign that your romantic intelligence needs improvement.

The Romantically Intelligent Approach to Conflict

Romantic intelligence is being aware at all times about what you're feeling, especially during arguments and crises. Your greater awareness means that you understand your behavior and feelings to such a degree that when problems arise in your relationship, they are understood clearly and handled directly. If you're not aware of your feelings, you cannot get along with others, and you certainly won't get along with your partner, at least not for very long.

A romantically intelligent relationship is a work in progress; improvement and growth never stop. This is what you and your partner need to understand for yourselves: that it's never to late to change yourselves to create a better relationship. If it's important enough for you, it is within your ability to create that better relationship; all you need is a willing partner to join you for the ride. It's more than worth it.

The Importance of Conflict Resolution

We cannot overemphasize the importance of conflict resolution in your relationship. Divorce statistics testify to the inability of most couples to be honest and courageous in their relationships. The need for honesty and courage holds true no matter what form your relationship takes, whether you are married or unmarried, straight or gay. The rules for romantic intelligence never change. The challenge is to stay aware, and to retain the openness to face yourself and assume some of the responsibility for what goes wrong with your relationship, as well as giving yourself the credit for making it a deeply felt, strongly committed, and cherishing love bond.

You must have enough emotional intelligence so that most problems in your relationship do not reoccur endlessly. If there is chronic strife because of reoccurring issues that are never handled effectively, your relationship will surely suffer. To gain some relief from your ongoing relationship stress and tensions, avoidance will become more important than honest problem-solving. As time goes on and dissatisfaction sets in, your relationship will become very unhappy, indeed.

The person with romantic intelligence is a problemsolver not a problem avoider. Although she doesn't welcome friction, she faces misunderstandings and conflicts squarely, knowing that they are an inevitable part of intimacy. She doesn't ignore, avoid, or minimize conflicts or issues with her partner; she tackles them head-on because she knows that avoidance creates distance and alienation. Neither does she take the opposite tack of exaggerating problems and issues. She is not a drama queen and her partner is not a drama king.

Anger and Rage

Many people are uncomfortable with powerful negative emotions like anger and rage. They do everything they can to avoid facing up to anger in either themselves or their partner. For the romantically intelligent couple, such emotions, although difficult and very troubling to face and deal with, are seen as a signals for problem-solving and for transforming their relationship.

Clearing the air is a prerequisite to closeness and intimacy. Avoiding the circumstances that create anger and rage leads only to distancing and estrangement from each other. For the committed romantically intelligent couple, it is their duty to work through troubling issues and distressing emotions. They know that such work is the prerequisite to sustaining their relationship and keeping it vibrant. They also know that problems of a personal nature outside their relationship are still both partners' concern and should be aired and solved, if that is what is needed and asked for.

Impulse Control

Finally, impulse control is a crucial element of conflict resolution: the ability to think before you act or to not act at all is the hallmark of romantic intelligence. Impulse control is critical to problem-solving; without it, a bad situation only gets worse and may irretrievably damage a relationship. With it, issues can be sorted out and resolved.

Ground Rules for Conflicts

Conflict provides the energy to solve problems, difficult issues, and impasses in relationships. Nevertheless, even if they are quarreling, the romantically intelligent couple does stick to certain ground rules to deal with misunderstandings and breakdowns in their relationship. Some of these ground rules follow.

★ Don't ignore issues by pretending they don't exist or are not very important because they seem insignificant to you.

★ Disclose what you're feeling and thinking in a way that doesn't push your partner's buttons.

★ Say what's troubling you, talk about what *you* feel about the situation, but don't find fault with your partner in a critical way. It only makes him or her defensive and will escalate the problem rather than solving it.

★ Separate (as best as you can) your personal issues from those of your partner or those of the relationship.

★ Understand that not every quarrel is a minefield or major battle.

★ Explore unspoken issues and understand that conflict, like dreams, involves displacement and denial. Many battles are fought over issues that have never been discussed openly, or issues that don't involve the relationship, but are one partner's own personal issues that have never been addressed or been brought into consciousness.

Resolving conflicts and finding solutions to the inevitable problems couples must face is not a natural talent; it must be learned and practiced. Many of us will go to extremes to avoid arguments and upsets. Others relish battles and enjoy the negative excitement. Such people are not happy unless there is an ongoing drama in their life. The bottom line is think before you act, come up with multiple solutions, stay positive, and take risks about saying what you are really feeling.

CHAPTER TEN

THE BRAVE NEW YOU AND ROMANTIC INTELLIGENCE

*We must never lose sight of the fact that people
and their needs are the only important consideration,
and not the preservation or initiation of any
particular style of life or of marriage.*

—James Leslie McCary

Persistence and emotional resiliency—the last two pillars of emotional intelligence—provide the foundation to stay the course. *Persistence* is the strength to not be blown off your path, but to trek on with grace and style, in spite of minor setbacks and major obstacles. *Emotional resiliency* is the ability to bounce back from major challenges, to navigate life's ups and downs with agility, and to understand that failures are disguised lessons for successful living. As a rule, these qualities are described as applying just to individuals, not to intimate relationships, but they are very pertinent to the success or failure of those relationships.

Romantic perseverance, the ability to steer a relationship through its natural course, involves knowing what to expect as the relationship proceeds, how to persist and not give up when it hits tough times, and how to motivate and coach each other during periods of personal challenge and growth. You discover and assess the pros and cons of your relationship: what it means to you, the reasons for its existence, why it should continue, or, perhaps, not continue. With perseverance, you learn to examine the romantically intelligent reasons to stay put in a relationship, and how to read the warning signs that maybe it's time to bail out.

Real Love Isn't a Romance Novel Plot

Life and love don't follow straight lines as in movie plots or romance novels. After Harry and Sally kiss and make up at the New Year's Eve party, their story doesn't end. Not only are there more plot twists and turns to come, there are hidden driveways, dangerous S-curves, roadblocks, traffic jams, crack-ups, and even avalanches that just keep on coming, especially at the most inconvenient times.

Unpredictability and the need for constant maneuvering are the prevailing rules of the relationship road. In the face of this reality, you can choose to be pessimistic and inflexible, or to panic and jump ship. You can exaggerate these realities, minimize them, try to control them, or deny them. In other words, you can take the emotionally unintelligent approach to the vicissitudes of love and life, or you can choose to exercise your romantic intelligence.

Choosing to persevere romantically will involve developing your inner resources and courage, and helping your partner to develop his or hers. On this road, you learn to cultivate a practical, optimistic attitude even while controlling overinflated, unrealistic optimism. That's the kind of cheery optimism where you let your imagination and expectations run so wild that it leaves you feeling let down and punched in the stomach, when things don't work out as you imagined they would.

If you learn how to hang in there and continue to practice what you learn, you will become skilled at talking about your feelings and motivating each other. In time, you will get the mortgage you want; in time, you will find the work situation you both want; and, in time, your in-laws will get over the fact that you took a Christmas vacation in Hawaii, instead of visiting them.

When you are persistent and emotionally resilient, you are open to constructive criticism from each other. You can separate your feelings from what you need to hear from your partner, as long as your partner talks to you in a respectful and caring way. Unconstructive criticism delivered in a harsh, judgmental tone can damage even good, solid relationships.

The Downhill Race

Love's course, at least course of love that lasts, is like a downhill ski race you win only after many years of trying. You get a significant boost at the starting gate as you push off and glide your way down to the first set of bumps. Then the hill gets steeper, the moguls icier, and the path between them narrows. It's harder to stick your pole into solid snow, and sometimes you miss altogether. Finally, after you turn and gyrate your way down the hill, the mountain smoothes out once again and you can breathe and cross the finish line. Staying the course takes guts, emotional flexibility, high self-esteem, and the will to succeed.

In romantic relationships, the bumps, moguls, and steep slides come from many, many sources including physical and emotional health issues, lack of money, raising children, in-law problems, sexual dysfunction, depression, boredom, problems with relatives and friends, spousal competition, and so forth. These issues and obstacles can throw you off course and into a cascading spill that leaves you on your knees. If you don't have the right kind of emotional and psychological equipment, you get stuck on the mountain. Sometimes you pull out of the race entirely. It's not that you haven't tried, but you realize, like Pat in the story that follows, that conditions on the hill will never improve.

Pat: A Romantically Intelligent Choice

Pat knew it was time to call her marriage quits after fourteen years of not being accepted for who she was. She felt totally alone in her marriage. She worried constantly about her future and even had nightmares about what would her life would be like when her two children were grown. "My marriage was a big empty pit. There was no emotional support. My husband never asked me once why I was unhappy, although he knew I was, because I expressed my sadness all the time." She believes her husband was afraid of learning the reason for her unhappiness, which was that she wanted more out of life. She wanted a partner who would encourage her potential to grow. When Pat told him that she wasn't the one for him, she knew their breakup would be tough on her financially and emotionally, but her integrity as a whole person was at stake.

Pat's decision followed many years of being invalidated by her partner. "My husband, Joel, never give me credit for my ideas until someone else affirmed them. Joel made fun of my 'spirituality' and my insistence that the kids not eat at McDonald's. He took the credit when I went back to nursing school and I became my graduating class's valedictorian. If we had dated another six months before we got married, it would never have happened."

Before Pat married Joel, she had been in a two-year relationship with Robert, of whom she says, "He was the only man I ever connected with on an emotional level. But he was from a different faith, and because he came from a very religious family, he ended the relationship." Pat remembers, "Being with Robert always made me be a better person."

After Robert ended their affair, Pat married Joel on the rebound. She went from a man with whom she could talk about anything to a man who never discussed anything that had to do with his emotions. Today, she has no regrets about leaving her marriage. Her independence and sense of self are intact. Some years back, she placed a call to the now happily married Robert. Their conversation confirmed her instincts about him being a fine, emotionally intelligent person. Even though she has occasional dates, she stays single. Pat has chosen to wait for another "Robert" to come into her life.

Romantically intelligent love requires each of you to think independently and feel autonomous: You understand your separate needs as well as the needs of the relationship. In Pat's case, she knew what romantically intelligent love could be like and was no longer willing to put up with a marriage in which her feelings, ideas, and spiritual life were not honored.

A relationship's staying power derives from each partner maintaining a unique, singular identity and emotional life. Each of you has your life and your inner world of feelings. You are aware when you lose part of yourself in a relationship; you know when your preferences and beliefs are respected and not judged; and you are sure about what you must do to remain whole and to preserve your identity.

EXERCISE: Assess Your Relationship

Now you must make an honest appraisal of your relationship. You may be alone by choice, as Pat is. You may be involved in an unsatisfying relationship where you quash your feelings and needs. Or you may be in a dynamic, mutually satisfying relationship where you can be yourself and express your feelings. Answering these questions may clarify some issues for you. As you do this exercise, pay attention to what emotions it evokes. This assignment is personal and not to be shared with anyone. Type or write everything that comes to your mind as you answer the questions, and record the feelings you experience with each thought or idea you write down.

It takes romantic intelligence to live with a partner and, sometimes, to live without one. With that in mind, now ask yourself the following questions:

1. Would you rather live with a partner who tells you how to think, how to be, and what to do, or with someone who calls on you to be strong, committed to your beliefs and principles, and to assert your independence?

2. Would you rather be alone or with someone who is threatened by your growth and the changes you have already made, and who holds you back from making further changes? Allie told us, "The bravest thing I ever did was to leave someone I loved because I knew he wasn't right for me. Now I'm alone and it's hard, but it was better than living a lie and raising false expectations in my partner."

3. Are you able to be open and honest with your partner? Can you agree to disagree on contentious issues and accept the other's point of view as having validity, too?

4. Do you see your relationship as a creative, mutual growth process?

5. Are you comfortable living on your own? Women who feel that they are not complete without a man, often discover when they are alone that another person does not solve their problems or make them complete. You are already complete within yourself.

6. Do you think you are better off with your partner than you would be on your own, because you share your feelings and problems?

7. How is your sense of self and your self-esteem? Are you as comfortable with your partner as you are alone?

8. Now, after you have answered the questions above to your satisfaction, make a list of all the aspects of your relationship that are worth fighting for. Are you having trouble thinking about what you value in your life with your partner? Or are the thoughts coming into your mind effortlessly? The rapidity or slowness of your thoughts are indicative of your degree of engagement and caring in your relationship.

Dodging the Punches and Toughing It Out

All relationships change with time: you grow older, your needs change, you see things differently, and life affects you in mysterious ways. You become wiser and more caring and compassionate, or you begin to be bitter. Your experiences may have caused you to become more callous and insensitive than you were when you began your adult life. At this point, the question you must ask yourself is this: Will you stay the victim of circumstances, clinging to bad situations and unsupportive relationships, or will you become self-directed and decide for yourself what kind of life to lead, and who to lead it with and love?

Using your romantic intelligence makes you braver, more willing to shine a light on own your face and on your relationship, to peer into your soul. Your romantic intelligence ignites your courage to be authentic with yourself and your partner, to risk disapproval, disagreements, criticism, and even rejection. The bravery of romantic intelligence allows you to ask yourself the following questions:

✯ Am I learning and growing with my partner?

✯ Am I a better person when I am with my partner?

✯ Are we successful in applying our romantic intelligence, and are we learning enough about each other to continue to be successful?

✯ Has living with my partner become like swallowing one bitter pill after another?

✯ Do we have the time, the motivation, and inclination to lift ourselves beyond "just settling" for our relationship as it is, instead of creating a truly extraordinary one?

Your Relationship Is in Trouble When. . . .

1. **Your relationship is in trouble when your once strong commitment is now weak.** Perhaps one (or both) of you is thinking twice about putting the time and energy into your relationship to make it work. The ties that bind make you feel resentful.

R IQ relationship: In relationships with high Romantic IQs, there is a strong commitment to each other and a healthy optimism that problems and issues can and will be discussed openly, and that solutions can be worked out. Both partners are willing to compromise on issues and meet each other halfway. They know that their partnership is central in their lives, and that when they have a problem that can't be solved—when compromise is not possible—then living with the problem without solving it may be a better choice than endangering their relationship.

In the romantically intelligent relationship, your commitment to your partner means you persevere—you don't give up when you reach an impasse with your partner. You both find a way to a solution that strengthens your relationship, a solution that may mean you agree to disagree.

2. Your relationship is in trouble when either one (or both) of you is unwilling to make personal changes for the sake of the relationship. You may feel that to make any personal changes is to admit fault and accept responsibility for the trouble you're having with your partner. When it is clear in your mind that your partner is to blame and that she or he alone should change if your relationship is to have a chance, then personal responsibility is lacking.

R IQ Relationship: Your relationship has a high Romantic IQ when you and your partner know that issues and problems are never one-sided affairs where one person is wrong and the other is right. You both have the courage to take responsibility for the problems in your relationship. You stay away from fault finding and assigning blame and instead you both recognize that there are differences in how you see and do things. You understand that to change for your partner and meet her or him at least halfway is not a sign of weakness and capitulation, most of the time.

Rather, the changes you make become your markers of personal growth and deeper security within your relationship. To both share responsibility and stay vulnerable to your partner can only bring you closer to each other. You don't disparage and criticize the other's character; you stick with the issues that need to be solved, and as empathetically good listeners, more times than not, you succeed.

3. Your relationship is in trouble when either one (or both) of you insist that the other is the problem. With this position you see no need to make any changes yourself instead; you require your partner to make all the changes for the relationship to work. If your partner doesn't do as you wish, your resentment grows and your unhappiness deepens.

R IQ relationship: When you or your partner agree to share at least some of the blame and responsibility when a problem arises, you don't move into polarized positions. You don't dig your heels in and focus on your partner as the culprit responsible for the latest misunderstanding or disagreement. To accept some of the heat forces a de-escalation of the conflict and an empathetic response from your partner. The foundation of this stance is the mutual trust that is integral to your relationship. With trust comes vulnerability; the two of you can expose your shortcomings and weak spots to each other, knowing that they won't be used against you but for you, to work out a solution.

4. Your relationship is in trouble when you're depressed and unhappy with yourself, and you expect your partner to say or do something that will make you happier. If you expect your partner to make up for what you lack in yourself, you put an unrealistic burden on your partner's shoulders, and you will experience repeated disappointments.

R IQ relationship: As someone with a high Romantic IQ, you know that your happiness is self-generated. Your partner cannot provide you with happiness. You can only activate that for yourself. Your partner can raise your spirits or provide you with encouragement to get to the bottom of your issues, but to be romantically intelligent is to personally create the circumstances that will bring fulfillment and satisfaction into your life. You share your happiness with your partner; you don't get it from him or her.

5. Your relationship is in trouble when your self-regard is low. Your self-esteem and self-respect are critical to how you feel about yourself, what you expect from your partner, and, in turn, how you treat your partner. If you don't understand or respect yourself, you will have a poor understanding of your impact on your partner; your problems will be a puzzle to you, and you will blame your partner for your unhappiness. You will fail to make healthy choices in your partnerships. Your relationships will reflect your lack of understanding and respect for yourself and, most importantly, you will seek partners who will feel about you the way you feel about yourself. In such a case, you will become angry when your partner mirrors your lack of self-regard back to you. If you don't feel good about yourself, don't expect your partner to feel good about you—not in the long term.

R IQ relationship: Your romantic intelligence shows itself in your positive self-regard, your acceptance of your whole self, and your understanding of your need to be self-protective. Your expectations of what you want from your partner—and what you give in return—derive from, depend on, and have everything to do with the mutual support you give to each other. This is the kind of support that nourishes the regard you feel for yourself, as well as the self-regard your partner feels for himself or herself. It is the kind of mutual support that encourages growth, change, individuality, and the freedom to think, choose, and do what is most meaningful to you, individually and together.

6. **You really know your relationship is in trouble when you and your partner are not growing and changing.** When one or both of you feels stuck, or in a rut, or when your relationship feels predictable, stale, and boring, when you are reluctant to grow and change, then you really are in trouble. When you (or your partner) are reluctant to grow or change, then one (or both) of you is exhibiting low romantic intelligence. In this kind of situation, you may even reinforce the reluctance to change in each other. But people change whether they want to or not.

Everything in nature is constantly changing and so are you. If you do not embrace change for yourself and your partner, eventually that leads to you not living up to your full potential, which can make you feel very unhappy indeed. Ultimately, it leads you to ask yourself, "Isn't there anything more to life than this?" If you or your partner restrict the other's yearnings, then resentment, anger, and hostility replace the hopes and dreams of a promising future together.

R IQ relationship: When high romantic intelligence is present, your partner encourages you to do what you want to do and to be who you want to be. This encouragement strengthens the bond of love you feel for each other because you feel supported and loved for what you do, who you are, and who you can become. And, of course, you give the same encouragement to your partner.

The Give Up and Go Syndrome

It takes *perseverance* and *courage* to get through all the inevitable issues you will face in your relationship. Some people give up too quickly; they would rather end the relationship than work on it. They are like gamblers who drop out of the game to cut their losses and run. When there are problems in their relationship, they see only two options: either their partner changes to improve the relationship, or they should leave. In most cases, it takes two people to make or break the relationship. In some cases, however, the responsibility for the failure of the breakup lies with only one person.

That person, usually, has little or no interest in learning much about his or her inner self. The less you know about yourself, your values, beliefs, likes, and dislikes—in short, what makes you tick—the greater the chances are that you will involve yourself yet again with a different person who, surprise, surprise, will present the same set of issues you had to deal with in your previous partnership, but chose not to by opting out of the relationship entirely. Not all partnerships work out and not all partnerships are meant to work out, and this applies whether you are romantically intelligent or not.

Transitional and Rebound Relationships

Some relationships serve a purpose and are important in a particular period in a person's life, but they serve no purpose after that period ends and they may become constraining and suffocating. For example, some rebound or transitional relationships will make you feel good about yourself while you still living with unresolved pain and anger. After a separation or divorce, transitional or rebound relationships can help to restore your self-confidence and heal your emotional scars. There's nothing wrong with such liaisons. They may be brief or long-term, based on mutual needs at the time, and they may serve their purpose.

Some people partner for the wrong reasons: to escape their parents' home, to settle a score with a past lover, to be with an unsuitable partner as an act of rebellion or way of declaring adulthood if you're young and immature. Some relationships have a short shelf life, while others, if both partners have high Romantic IQs, continue for years and years, until one partner dies. Sometimes two people come together in a match that was "made in heaven," until one partner becomes even more romantically intelligent and the other one does not. People change and the rules change; without flexibility and the ability to accommodate and support those changes, the relationship disintegrates and dies.

People don't always grow closer together, but they do grow apart. To be romantically intelligent is to persevere and be flexible with your partner, and resilient in the face of the changes, surprises, and even shocks that will take place in your partnership. However, to persevere when all the avenues to improve the relationship have failed is foolish. That is the time to use your bravery, perseverance, and resilience to move out of the relationship and on with your life.

If you're living in a relationship that has come to a dead end and you are very unhappy, you should not waste your time and energy being stuck your bad situation. If you blame your partner for the situation, and you hold him or her responsible for your happiness, that can only increase your resentment and hostility. If you feel that your spirit is dying and you cannot grow and live your life as you see fit, you must leave—you must change your life.

Living in partnership with someone who has a low Romantic IQ will cause you to feel trapped and paralyzed. When you feel you have no choices or you are afraid to make choices to free yourself, all of the unpleasant elements of the relationship become intensified. It is true that some people have such an enormous fear of being alone that they would rather suffer and have their spirits broken in poor relationships than take the risk of liberating themselves to create new possibilities by leaving and starting anew. For many people, making the choice to leave someone can be like climbing Everest. Yet those who do make the climb, inch by painful inch, may find their true selves and, eventually, true love at the summit.

To be romantically intelligent is to understand that if your relationship ends, it's not necessarily a sign of failure. More likely it is a sign of growth, because when you respect yourself enough to end an unhappy relationship, the likelihood is that you expect to be treated better the next time. You want to give your love to someone who will welcome it and give you love and support in return.

Here are some useful statements to say to yourself when your relationship is ending after all efforts to save it have failed.

1. I always feel unhappy when I am with my partner, no matter how much time we spend together.

2. I want to spend most of my time alone, away from my partner, even if I've spent little time with him or her during the week.

3. I can cut the tension between the two of us with a knife. I find relief from this tension only when I am away from my partner.

4. I feel emotionally distant from my partner, and not only doesn't this worry me, I'm also not motivated to do anything about it.

5. I spend more time thinking about getting out of my relationship than staying in it, especially after our last argument.

6. I don't trust my partner, and whatever he or she says or does, doesn't convince me otherwise.

7. My partner abuses alcohol and drugs. He or she won't get help and denies there is a problem. I can't put up with this any longer.

8. The thought of growing old with my partner frightens and depresses me.

9. I'm not interested in telling my partner what I am thinking or feeling, because it just doesn't matter anymore.

10. I feel as if I'm living with a stranger. What did I ever see in him or her in the first place?

11. I feel that my partner and I are like "two ships in the night" just passing through. I don't care what he or she thinks or feels anymore.

12. I feel numb. I no longer even get annoyed with my partner's obnoxious behavior.

13. I fantasize about my partner being gone far away, or even dead (that's one way of getting rid of him or her and finding some relief for myself).

Not all relationships end with a great deal of noise, drama, and conflict. Some end quietly, when one or both partners decide that it's time, the relationship has run its course. As said above, the end of a relationship is not failure, but the acknowledgement that the relationship cannot go any further.

When a relationship ends, it is very useful to think about the time and the effort you put into it. It is helpful to remember the happiness and good times you had with your partner. Your memories may cause you to feel pain, but you will gain a greater understanding of yourself and why you were with that partner. When you were happy together was a successful time. To view your entire relationship as a failure because it had to end is to ignore the successes you did achieve within the relationship. Remember, to keep a relationship going for fear of not being able to rely on your own resources is the greatest failure of them all.

Exercising your romantic intelligence will tell you the course to take, your courage and perseverance will drive you, and you will continue to experience success in life and in love. You can learn to look back without regrets, but with an appreciation for all that you've been through. You will know that your life is a life well lived, and that you are learning how to be as smart in love as you are in your life.

♥

As we conclude this book, our hope is that you will risk getting closer to your partner, that you will dare to know yourself, and that you will mobilize your emotions to support each other's growth and separate journeys. Whether you are in a relationship or not, you will remain the brave new you—someone who can embrace pleasure and deal with pain, who knows about the onset of love, its loss, and the enduring love that flows from being honest about your feelings with yourself and others. Treasure your self-respect, honor your intuitions. We wish you romantically intelligent love, passion, and the capacity to experience compassion for others.

REFERENCES

Austen. J. 1998 [1811]. *Sense and Sensibility*. Oxford: Oxford University Press.

Barnett, R., and C. Barnett. 2001. Women, men, work, and family: A Janet Sibley Hyde expansionist theory. *American Psychologist* 56(10):781-796.

Blumstein, P., and P. Schwartz. 1983. *American Couples*. New York: William Morrow.

Branden, N. 1997. *The Art of Living Consciously: The Power of Awareness to Transform Everyday Life*. New York: Simon & Shuster, Fireside Book.

Fisher, H. 1992. *Anatomy of Love:The Mysteries of Mating, Marriage, and Why We Stray*. New York: Faucett Columbine.

Freud, S. 1971. The wolf man. In *The Wolf-Man by the Wolf-Man: The Double Story of Freud's Most Famous Case*, edited by Muriel Gardner. New York: Basic Books.

Goleman, D. 1997. *Emotional Intelligence: Why It Matters More than IQ*. New York: Bantam Books.

Guardian. 2000. "American Beauty." Friday, January 28, 2000. *The Guardian*, Guardian Unlimited, http://filmguardian.co.UK/Guardian/0,6961,00.html.

Hatfield, E. 1989. Passionate and compassionate love. In *The Psychology of Love*, edited by R. J. Sternberg and M. L. Barnes. New Haven: Yale University Press.

Hatfield, E., and R. Rapson. 1993. Love and attachment processes. In *Handbook of Emotions*, edited by M. Lewis and J. Haviland. New York: Guilford Press.

Hawthorne, N. 1959 [1853]. *The Scarlet Letter*. New York: Signet.

Lewis, M., and J. M. Haviland, eds. 1993. *Handbook of Emotions*. New York: Guilford Press.

Liebowitz, M. 1993. Love and attachment process. In *Handbook of Emotions*, edited by M. Lewis and J. Haviland. New York: Guilford Press.

Fisher, H. 1992. *Anatomy of Love: The Mysteries of Mating, Marriage, and Why We Stray*, by H. Fisher. New York: Faucett Columbine.

Maheu, M., R. Subotnick, and S. Glass. 2001. *Infidelity on the Internet: Virtual Relationships and Real Betrayal*. New York: Sourcebooks Trade.

McLaren, K. 2001. *Emotional Genius: Discovering the Deepest Language of the Soul*. Columbia, California: Laughing Tree Press.

———. 2002. *Emotional Genius: Discovering the Deepest Language of the Soul*. Audiotapes. Chicago: Nightingale Conant.

Myss, C. 1996. *Anatomy of the Spirit: The Seven Stages of Power and Healing*. New York: Three Rivers Press.

Philippon, D. 2002. Ecologies of love: An interview with Barry Lopez. *Ruminator Review*, No. 12, Winter 2002-2003, pages 22-23.

Plutchik, R. 1993. Emotions and their vicissitudes: Emotions and psychopathology. In *Handbook of Emotions*, edited by M. Lewis and J. M. Haviland. New York: Guilford Press.

Scott, S. 1999. *Simple Steps to Impossible Dreams: The 15 Power of Secrets of the World's Most Successful People*. New York: Simon & Schuster.

Segal, J. 1997. *Emotional Intelligence: A Practical Guide to Harnessing the Power of Your Instincts and Emotions*. New York: Holt.

Shaughnessy, M. F., and P. Shakesby. 1992. "Adolescent sexual and emotional intimacy." *Adolescence* 27(106):475-480.

Stendhal, B. 1926. *The Red and the Black*. Translated by C. K. Scott-Moncrieff, New York: Liverright.

Sternberg, R. J., and M. L. Barnes. 1988. *The Psychology of Love*. New Haven: Yale University Press.

Tennov, D. 1979. *Love and Limerence: The Experience of Being in Love*. Second edition. New York: Scarborough.

———. 1989. Quoted in *The Psychology of Love*, edited by R. J. Sternberg and M. L. Barnes. New Haven: Yale University Press.

Viscott, D. 1987. *I Love You, Let's Work It Out*. New York: Pocket Books.

———. 1996. *Emotional Resilence: Simple Truths for Dealing with the Unfinished Business of Your Life*. New York: Crown Publishers.

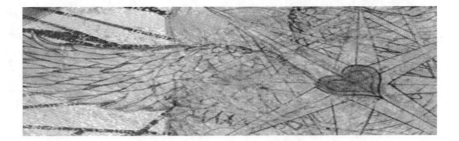

CONTACT US

Mary and John Valentis would like to hear from you about your experiences in working to achieve romantically intelligent relationships. Please contact them at their Web site www.bravenewyou.net.

Mary and John offer workshops and seminars based on the principles and practices presented in this book and their previous one, *Brave New You: 12 Dynamic Strategies for Saying What You Want and Being Who You Are*. These programs are appropriate for individuals, couples, health professionals, and those interested in personal development, in becoming emotionally brave, and in achieving intimate relationships that last.

—Mary and John Valentis, Ph.D.'s

Mary Valentis, Ph.D., teaches writing, literature, popular culture, and literary theory at the State University of New York at Albany. She began her writing career as a reporter and columnist for the Hearst Newspapers after graduating with honors from Connecticut College. Coauthor of *Brave New You: 12 Dynamic Strategies for Saying What You Want and Being Who You Are, Female Rage: Unlocking Its Secrets, Claiming Its Power,* and editor of *The American Sublime,* Valentis has published numerous articles in such magazines as *New Woman* and in scholarly journals and collections. She lectures and consults widely both here and in Europe. Her classes, retreats, and workshops focus on women's issues, romantic love, trauma writing, and popular culture.

John Valentis, Ph.D., has been involved in the mental-health field since 1975. Dr. Valentis has an independent practice in clinical hypnosis and psychotherapy and specializes in motivation, relationships, and the psychology of health. The host of radio station WALE's *The Dr. John Valentis Show,* a call-in advice program, he has been a sought after guest on national and local television. He presents training seminars on various mental-health issues and skill enhancement for physicians and mental-health practitioners.

Some Other
New Harbinger Titles

Helping Your Depressed Child, Item 3228 $14.95

The Couples's Guide to Love and Money, Item 3112 $18.95

50 Wonderful Ways to be a Single-Parent Family, Item 3082 $12.95

Caring for Your Grieving Child, Item 3066 $14.95

Helping Your Child Overcome an Eating Disorder, Item 3104 $16.95

Helping Your Angry Child, Item 3120 $17.95

The Stepparent's Survival Guide, Item 3058 $17.95

Drugs and Your Kid, Item 3015 $15.95

The Daughter-In-Law's Survival Guide, Item 2817 $12.95

Whose Life Is It Anyway?, Item 2892 $14.95

It Happened to Me, Item 2795 $17.95

Act it Out, Item 2906 $19.95

Parenting Your Older Adopted Child, Item 2841 $16.95

Boy Talk, Item 271X $14.95

Talking to Alzheimer's, Item 2701 $12.95

Helping a Child with Nonverbal Learning Disorder or Asperger's Syndrome, Item 2779 $14.95

The 50 Best Ways to Simplify Your Life, Item 2558 $11.95

When Anger Hurts Your Relationship, Item 2604 $13.95

The Couple's Survival Workbook, Item 254X $18.95

Loving Your Teenage Daughter, Item 2620 $14.95

The Hidden Feeling of Motherhood, Item 2485 $14.95

Parenting Well When You're Depressed, Item 2515 $17.95

Thinking Pregnant, Item 2302 $13.95

Call toll free, **1-800-748-6273,** or log on to our online bookstore at **www.newharbinger.com** to order. Have your Visa or Mastercard number ready. Or send a check for the titles you want to New Harbinger Publications, Inc., 5674 Shattuck Ave., Oakland, CA 94609. Include $4.50 for the first book and 75¢ for each additional book, to cover shipping and handling. (California residents please include appropriate sales tax.) Allow two to five weeks for delivery.

Prices subject to change without notice.